THE TEACHING FOR SOCIAL JUSTICE SERIES, *continued*

BEING BAD

My Baby Brother and the School-to-Prison Pipeline

Crystal T. Laura

Foreword by William Ayers
Afterword by Erica R. Meiners

TEACHERS COLLEGE PRESS

TEACHERS COLLEGE | COLUMBIA UNIVERSITY
NEW YORK AND LONDON

Published by Teachers College Press, 1234 Amsterdam Avenue, New York, NY
10027

Library of Congress Cataloging-in-Publication Data

Laura, Crystal T.
    Being bad : my baby brother and the school-to-prison pipeline / Crystal T.
    Laura ; foreword by William Ayers ; afterword by Erica R. Meiners.
        pages cm. — (The teaching for social justice series)
    Includes bibliographical references and index.
    ISBN 978-0-8077-5596-9 (pbk. : alk. paper)
    ISBN 978-0-8077-5597-6 (hardcover : alk. paper)
    ISBN 978-0-8077-7339-0 (ebook)
        1. African American boys—Education—Social aspects. 2. African American
    young men—Education—Social aspects. 3. African American high school
    students—Illinois—Biography. 4. School discipline—United States. 5. Chicago
    Public Schools. 6. Juvenile justice, Administration of—United States. I. Title.
    LC2779.L38   2014
    371.829'96073—dc23   2014028036

ISBN 978-0-8077-5596-9 (paper)
ISBN 978-0-8077-5597-6 (hardcover)
ISBN 978-0-8077-7339-0 (ebook)

Printed on acid-free paper
Manufactured in the United States of America

21 20 19 18 17   8 7 6 5 4 3

Contents

Foreword

IMET CHRIS SMITH through a thick plexiglass window, each of us scrunched onto a small metal stool and taking turns shouting hellos and introductions through a little metal grate in order to be heard above the din. Chris was incarcerated in Cook County Jail awaiting trial on a robbery charge, and I was visiting because I'd promised Crystal Laura, his sister and my student at the time, as well as my friend then and now, that I would. The place was miserable: a dark and narrow hallway with maybe 15 of us visitors evenly distributed on our side of the impenetrable glass and concrete wall, waiting. We'd inched along the slow-snaking roped-off security line; we'd been run through metal detectors and then patted down; we'd been identity-checked and hand-stamped; we'd been ordered about, checked off, and registered; some of us had even been scolded by the turn-keys for our choice of pants or top and been banished, told to come back wearing "appropriate" clothing. After all that I thought for sure we'd be meeting in a big room seated at tables across from our friends or loved ones. No such thing: Chris and the other cuffed and chained Black men shuffled in and took seats on their side of the barrier, straining to be seen and heard. The stench of the slave market was everywhere.

"What's up?" I shouted, and he smiled and shouted back: "Doing good; nice to meet you." He was as Crystal had always described him: sharp, smiling, small in his jumbo-sized jump suit, and "cute as a button."

With this courageous book Crystal Laura takes us on an odyssey into her cherished little brother's world—jail and prison to be sure, but before that school and special education, the temptations and the perils of the streets, and right from the start a beloved family fighting with all its might to disrupt a narrative with its brutal conclusion seemingly already written in indelible ink for Chris. With an ethnographer's endurance, a scholar's intent, and a sister's hopeful heart, Crystal Laura has constructed a unique and morally awake narrative of the twists and turns that confront kids like Chris everyday in every corner of America. There are surprises and insights on every page, lessons for teachers, parents, youth workers, and anyone concerned about the sorry state we're in regarding the future of young men of color.

Dr. Crystal Laura calls herself a "sister/scholar," and that hybrid classification seems exactly right. Her writing ambitions are thoroughly linked to her deepest ethical ambitions—she is practicing the discipline of the heart. She is also practicing the discipline of the mind, willing to follow every lead, pursue every twist and turn in a relentless search for why things are as they are; the inspiration is entirely authentic: "I don't know" and I must find out because our very lives depend on it. She knows clearly what she is writing for and what she's writing against, what she hopes to change and combat, affirm and illuminate by entering this work into the public square. Far from a weakness, passionate regard and sisterly scholarship are a singular strength here.

She's a gifted storyteller for sure, and her writing and research are anti-systematic, experimental, creative and generative, free from the violence of dogma and self-righteousness. This is a search and a struggle to make sense—and we can actually witness and become a party to that struggle on the page—a journey, not by a tourist, but by a pilgrim.

In school Chris eventually became a magnet for labels, and branded, the markers follow him around like flies, sometimes hemming him in, other times mocking him. He was inspected and appraised often, corrected and reformed regularly. Eventually the labels take over—he becomes his manila envelope and cumulative file, the sum of his statistical profile in the estimation of the institution—and the family desperately pursues contradictory strategies. Barbara, his fierce and formidable mother, decided to tentatively embrace an inadequate label hoping it would bring the promised focus and services; Crystal reached for her books and research papers to contextualize the situation and frame the personal in the social. But Chris wasn't having any of it; he rejected both the psychological and the sociological. The alternative for him was logical: "I messed up. I have to take responsibility." Chris resists the deficit theory, refuses the easy pathologizing of his circumstances, wanting his own agency and will to count for something. "Nothing about us without us" chant the disability activists today, and Chris echoes that sentiment.

I'm reminded of a headline from the *Onion*, a journal of humor and satire that warns of a growing epidemic among children: "An estimated 20 million U.S. children," it asserts, are believed to suffer from a "poorly understood neurological condition called YTD, or Youthful Tendency Disorder." The article details the early warning signs of YTD, including sudden episodes of shouting and singing, conversations with imaginary friends, poor impulse control with regard to sugared snacks, preferring playtime and flights of fancy to schoolwork, and confusing oneself with animals and objects like airplanes. An imaginary mother whose child was recently diagnosed with YTD expresses guarded relief: "At least we know we weren't bad parents," she says hopefully. "We simply had a child who was born with a medical disorder."

This scrap of satire works because it offers a fractured-mirror image of what's actually happening, both in and outside of schools: Children have become the objects of an all-pervasive and extremely toxic barrage of labels and stereotypes, their humanity terribly reduced in the process, their three-dimensional realities diminished, and their lived experiences eclipsed. We are surely headed for some brave new world of forced uniformity, unique mechanisms of disciplinary surveillance, obligatory obedience, and compulsory conformity. We can see the school-to-prison pipeline looming large.

And prison it is. With millions of our fellow citizens living in cages and vanishing behind walls, a host of social problems and challenges are buried but not faced, and surely not solved. Poverty, unemployment, illiteracy, failing schools, homelessness, inadequate health care, substance abuse and addiction, mental illness—these are all within our power to answer, but only when we are willing to take an essential first step: opening our eyes and making an honest accounting of the human costs and the human possibilities before us.

Being Bad is a powerful tool in that effort. Intimate and intense, this unique work of memoir, history, and critical theory is filled with anguish, conflict, and contradiction—a place many of us inhabit but few are willing to expose so bravely. Crystal Laura helps all of us recognize the urgency of our work with young people and the responsibility we share in educating them.

In a lucid and entirely compelling conclusion Crystal Laura invites us to join hands with her and become part of the solution: Listen to children and youth; protect them and challenge them; embrace them with generosity and hope. Her vision of teaching with love and joy and justice hits hard because we know how hard-earned that revelation is.

Faith, hope, and love abide, these three; and the greatest of these is love.

—William Ayers

Preface

DEAR READER, what you are holding is the record of a conversation I needed to have with myself that you will be better for overhearing. It's about my little brother, Chris, whom I love crazily and whom, until I wrote this book, I only pretended to understand. We are separated by a lot of things, including almost a decade in age. Chris is in his early 20s now, a young Black man, and, in my biased opinion, cute as a button. Unless I said so, you would never know that Chris is waiting to be tried in connection with crimes for which he could spend a big chunk of his 30s, 40s, 50s, and even 60s locked up. I have made a point to selectively forget what I have heard about the circumstances of his arrest. Chris has been out of jail on bail for over a year now and we have not—and probably will not—discuss whatever he did or did not do. That is for Chris and his lawyers to sort out. What I have been asking myself over and over again is how in the world my brother got into such a mess to begin with, and what, if anything, someone could have done to keep him out of it. These questions have been bothering me, and sensing that this is not quite the right time to bring up the topic with Chris, I decided to deal with the problem by writing into it.

My search for clues about the course of Chris' life took me from the urgency of the god-awful moment, backward and forward through raw recollections of his childhood, to bodies of scholarship, and up against the simple facts I have come by along the way: (1) that what happened with him was a completely preventable tragedy, and (2) that being squeezed between the tensions of education and schooling had everything to do with how his story took shape. The details of his story, and the inner conflicts that I have experienced in trying to tell it with both candor and compassion, are what you will find in the next hundred pages or so.

Before forging ahead, I should admit that *Being Bad* almost did not make it into your hands. Writing a personal essay that would help me think through the individual choices and broader structures that took down my baby brother is one thing; publishing such an intimate piece for a skeptical audience is quite another. Why the hesitation? Well, because I am a woman who worries, and because certain hypothetical situations have begged me to reconsider sharing. I suppose being misconstrued is an assumed risk when you decide to say exactly what's on your mind. Still, I would hate for anything I have written to be twisted to support discourses of damage and deviance; in other words, as evidence that Chris and, by extension, a whole bunch of other folks really are "bad." Way too much of that literature is going around spreading lies about people, families, and communities, especially those of color. I have tried to be fair—neither portraying Chris as a powerless victim nor as a superhero—and also intentional about describing both his local narrative and concentric circles of contexts. But, just in case, let me be upfront: Using my anecdotes as examples of pathology or as confirmation that anyone lies in a bed totally of his or her own making not only misses the point, but is just wrong.

Introducing you to my brother was intended to help you think deeply and maybe even differently about how youth like him fall through the cracks. I know I do. Chris and I grew up together, but I recall actually paying him close attention right around the time I left home for college, when the word was that he had been acting a plum fool at his middle school. His grades were slipping. He'd become less interested in the gazillion extracurricular activities he once enjoyed. He suddenly had a filthy mouth. In the beginning, Chris was given the dispensation of being a teenager, but when there was more of the same quarter after quarter, his teachers and we in the family started looking for other explanations. The easiest to grab onto was that he either couldn't or wouldn't learn. That helped us stage some short-term interventions and find peace for a minute. My brother, though, never bought it; Chris bucked the deficit theory as if he were fighting for his life. It didn't occur to me until much, much later that really he was, and that the story of his struggle needed to be captured and spread like wildfire.

But that raises another bothersome possibility of bringing what I wrote from the cloister of my underwear drawer to bookshelves: What if I haven't struck a proper balance between the need to relay the lessons that Chris' cautionary tale teaches and how my family feels about being exposed? Several measures were put in place to deal with this very issue, such as deleting overly sensitive material, giving family members copies of drafts for their feedback, getting their permission to go public with the revised drafts that we agree are insightful but not a tell-all, and keeping them up-to-date with whatever stage of development the book was in. No one has yet expressed discomfort or regret. But the lack of anonymity, among other irresolvable ethical issues, often makes me nervous. In my head, I have a fiction version of this book, in which the protagonist is a composite character of Chris and other kids who carry the messages I am drawing out here. The idea, of course, is that the made-up Chris protects the real Chris and the people who care about him from the writing and from the world's two cents. When I pitched the idea of the book to Chris, he argued in favor of sticking to the original script, reminding me that making up even parts of the story would subtract from its authenticity as proof that he exists, which is central to the issue of invisibility and marginalization that the book takes up.

Being Bad explores other big-picture issues, as well—the under-education of Black males, the place and importance of scapegoats in our culture, the on-the-ground reality of zero tolerance, the role of mainstream media in constructing Black masculinity, the relationships between schools and prisons—what I call the "social ecology of discipline." I will show you what I mean in a bit, but suffice it to say that, for certain youth, there is a clear pathway to jails and prisons, and it is connected to the social and academic institutions they navigate daily.

Every now and then, I am embarrassed—not by my brother, but by the fact that he went through the pipeline with so many well-educated, heavily involved, unsuspecting adults around him. This, too, nudged me to reevaluate publishing the book for you. How can I hope that anyone, particularly anyone in the field of education, will be encouraged to learn more in order to do more when they see how painful and hard it was for me to figure out what was up with someone in my own home? Or, what if getting to the bottom of things seems too laborious and you, the reader, chalk this up as a private matter unrelated to any of your business? Recently, I went to my mother, Barbara, who is one of those glass-half-full types, for her thoughts on these questions. Let me relay to you what she told me: that we have nothing to be ashamed of; that personal problems tend to be rooted in larger, more elusive conditions; that keeping them quiet not only does little by way of change but it eats away at those with the secrets; and that my job as a writer, a teacher, a mother, and a sister is to always remember these thoughts. Point taken. Having found the words, the nerve, and the support to press "Send," I finally did. And now the book and its nuggets of our truth—as partial as they may be—are all yours.

Onward.

CHAPTER 1

My Brother, Chris

W HEN PEOPLE GET CAUGHT UP in the school-to-prison pipeline, it means they have been poorly educated, prepped for dead-end jobs, the streets, and permanent detention; they have been systematically screwed. Take my brother, Chris. Out on bail, Chris is so far gone that he's been telling folks he's not only ready to return to jail, but is actually anxious to start living his life there. I can't understand why anybody would be in a hurry to do a whole lot of nothing inside the time trap. But I'm guessing that when you're all of 21 years old and looking to spend the next half century locked up, the sooner you get on with it, the better.

A young Black man with five felony cases open and hanging overhead is done for. I should just throw my hands up and admit it. My brother is clinically depressed and trying to solve a nasty drug problem by binge drinking. The throes of the pipeline have literally made him sick.

Don't get me wrong. I am not so bold about this in his face. These past 5 years—ever since Chris dropped out of high school—I have felt in my nerves that something awful would happen, but I've mostly kept this subterranean sense to myself. It is not that I see what's happening with my brother as a private matter or as a shameful family secret. I have written about Chris. I've wandered my way through a dissertation and speculated in articles printed for an audience of academics. My graduate students have heard my brother's story, and many of my colleagues teaching in universities across the country know a little something about him, too. But my concern is this: At home, I've noticed a hesitance to offer my unfiltered opinions, a kind of throat clearing in my conversations with Chris, an inability to cut the underbrush and speak. When I am around him, I busy myself with the smallest of tasks, and, during the time we are alone together, I question him clumsily, to avoid the quiet moment that may invite me to say what I think. For my brother's part, bless his heart, he seems to enjoy being the center of attention. There is a hint of guilt nagging me, though, if only at the fact that I have shared things with near strangers that I can't seem to explain to someone I care about deeply. Chris' days of freedom are numbered, and my inclination is to bluff until they are through because unstinting honesty won't do him any good right now.

Yet, a big part of me wants to chuck this easy resolution and ask who the bad boy is that Chris has become. How'd he get to this wretched place? And why am I stuttering over it? I want to know. All the time that I have been worrying about Chris—and doing it cock-eyed, with the bifocal lenses of both sister and scholar—it has only recently occurred to me to sit my butt in a chair and confront him directly. I suspect that the heat of the furnace we're in has brought me, as usual, to the page first. What I know is that there's a story here—not just about my brother but about huge, crashing issues—and I just need to get it straight.

★   ★   ★

Some people are so animated that any chance encounter with them promises a decent show. My brother used to be like that: uninhibited, shamelessly expressive, bounding with energy. It didn't take much to wind him up and watch him go. But lately, I have seen less and less of that Chris. Today's Chris has a fettered calm about him, a preoccupation with the worst possible scenario, and a tendency to slip into a brooding, pensive stare.

I can remember seeing that look on Chris a while ago, when he wrapped his used Pontiac around a light pole while cruising the city sloppy drunk. After the accident, paramedics put Chris in a neck brace and backboard and rushed him to the nearest ER. At first, Chris wouldn't say who he was and what had happened that night, but the doctor said that when she arrived, he was beyond control—cursing nurses out, using the secretary's phone, bleeding all over everything. The doctor called security and, because Chris was just a teenager, security called my mother. Mom sped across town to the hospital—at 3:00 A.M.—where she found Chris scraped and bruised, strapped to a bed with four-point restraints. Chris was released to the police, who let him go home to sober up. I came by later that afternoon just as the hangover, the throbbing pain, and the reality of things were all beginning to set in: He'd almost wiped himself out, had damaged public property, badgered the help, and totaled his first car. He had received the car less than 24 hours before, as a reward for the recent stretch of time in which he'd managed to stay out of trouble. Wearing that concentrated gaze, he said, "I tweaked," which, in his characteristic vernacular, translates loosely to "I messed up."

That pitiful stare is as telling and unforgettable as a bad dream. He's put it on again and again at every court appearance and during every jailhouse visit. Without fail, that look makes me want to wail out loud. Once, in June 2012, the year my second child was born, I did just that. I was 9 months pregnant and, as is typical for a woman in that condition, I was hot and bothered, in and out of hormonal fits. I was also too wary of going into labor inside the dungeon—that is, Cook County Jail, or "the County"—to show up alone. So there we were, my husband, Jelani, and I, sitting behind a glass partition (after we'd been X-rayed, searched, and IDed by a gaggle of guards two or three times over), waiting for Chris to toddle in. Jelani checked his watch. He'd gotten in the habit of keeping tabs on the length of our visits, which were supposed to last a measly half hour (a few minutes more, if we were lucky), but often we got much less. It was 5:00. By now, I thought, Chris' friends who had visited earlier should be midway home and my sister should be climbing into her car to make the schlep down here. We were spread out exactly as planned.

It was a hard lesson learning to coordinate visiting days. The year before, when Chris picked up his first case, my sister, my mother, and I went to the County to see about him. All the way up the Bishop

Ford and Dan Ryan freeways, we said no more than a few words—we were all probably fantasizing about wringing his scrawny neck, as piping mad as we were. But when we arrived, taken aback by the whole situation, we agreed on the spot to stagger repeated visits in a constant rotation, to hang around the place all day long if it meant we could keep him with us and out of his cell. I can recall Mom sharing our arrangement with the set of guards who took our registration.

"It doesn't work like that," the big one chuckled. As soon as he said this, I realized that we were making a rookie mistake, proposing accommodations as if we were checking in at some highfalutin hotel. He dismissed it outright: "You came together, you'll see him together."

My sister, Andrea, smacked her lips, my belly flopped, and my mother instantly turned red in the face. She tried explaining that we were new to the County, pleading—quietly, cautiously—for an exception.

The little guard was nicer. He said, "I'm sorry, Miss, but there's nothing we can do." Annoyed, we huddled up and sketched the logistics of returning again the very next day. "Um," he butted in, "unfortunately, you can't come back for another week."

There is no dignity in jailhouse visits, and the first one is the worst. All that fear and frustration you've been harboring does not well up at the time of the arrest. No, not until you are trying to work the system—to navigate the impersonal, impenetrable gulag—does it take every fiber of you to keep from going off. But I doubt that's what I was thinking about at that moment. I was almost certainly picturing Chris, scared witless. He was 18 then—9 years younger than me. Lanky, with wide eyes like saucers. Funny, artistic, and sweet as pie. Easy pickings, for sure. When his name was called, we hurried toward the line forming outside the visiting room and filed in, cooperatively.

★   ★   ★

Somewhere between my introduction to County and this last time that I waddled into it, I discovered a couple of more unstated givens:

One, the term *visiting room* is a euphemism. The room—a congested hallway, really—seems to narrow with reckless determination that makes it hard to breathe. Whenever I'm inside, I instantly feel myself losing a sense of proportion, squeezed between the expanse of cement walls and stools bolted to the floor. Two, the stools tucked in the see-through cubicles on either end of the hallway are prime real estate, desirable because of their relative privacy, which, given the context, is obviously a valued comfort. Regulars know to rush for them, snag one, and stay put. That's just what Jelani and I did.

After 5 or 6 minutes, in shuffled a crush of banana yellow jumpsuits. The color is important. Had they been dressed in khaki, there would have been nothing remarkable to set them apart from the hundreds of other men under maximum security in my brother's division. But yellow is special, reserved for those in "PC" or protective custody; it screams for undue notice. For safety, Chris had asked to be separated from the general population, then changed his mind when he crossed paths with a guy in khaki who called him a snitch, and changed it again when someone on his deck was stabbed to death. PC was perhaps the lesser of two evils, but besides having a questionable reputation, the label brought with it a mixed bag. The "perk," for lack of a better word, was extra time bunkered in a cell.

This is not to be confused with "seg," or disciplinary segregation, colloquially known as the hole. Apparently, that's a whole other situation. Chris once wrote me: "I don't know if you came to see me but im in the hole. I can't get any phone calls, i don't know bout visits. I gotta be here for 10 days. It aint no joke down here crys. I can't leave the cell for showers or nothin and its drivin me crazy!!!" And toward the end of the note, "I'm surrounded by killers and rapists . . . I don't fit in here."

There were eight brothers in yellow, all of them Black, and most around Chris' age. Chris, as always, took forever to appear. I bobbed from side to side—peeking over and through the crowd, waving my hands wildly—to make sure he knew he had company. Was I over the top? Sure, but as far as I am concerned, it was a necessary distraction. I have seen people—both inmates and visitors—come and go without connecting with one another. Blame those unfortunate occurrences on processing errors or maybe poor timing, but every now and then, somebody's son was left standing idly by, sick, scanning the room for his absent lifeline to the engaged world, while the rest of us chummed it up.

It was loud, understandably, with so many full-blown conversations happening all at once, and everybody trying to outdo everybody else. In the movies, there is a phone—an icky, worn-out phone, but a phone nonetheless. Here, we have a tiny, metal-grated opening in Plexiglas a good distance from a stool, which means that unless you're 6 feet tall and rail thin, like Chris (and quite unlike me), then sitting and chatting is nearly impossible. When Chris settled down, I stood and, folding over a ballooning midsection, brought my lips close enough to the speaker to kiss it. The rest was largely routine. I drew him out, asking him how he was doing, about the latest in the County, whether he had thought of a slick name for the baby, if he needed any books or money in his account. And when I ran out of steam, Jelani took the baton, keeping the exchange going.

Two things stick out in my memory from this visit: The first is that Chris had on a short-sleeved T-shirt underneath his County-issued digs, with his tattoos (the ones that churned my stomach to find out he'd recently gotten), in full view. He hid them, with a long thermal top even in the warmth of a summer swelter, before only the most important people: his judge and our mother. He hid them from the judge so as not to feed any inflamed attitudes that would have colored his day in court. He hid them from Mom because he knew good and well that being a grown man in the protective custody of the police wouldn't save him from her wrath. But today was Tuesday, and my mother's visits were consistently bright and early on Saturday mornings. Jelani and I did not have such powerful reach anyway, so Chris could skip the song and dance with us.

The other thing I remember is the good-bye, a sappy scene filled with such ritual and drama it could have been plucked right out of one of those prison documentaries. A guard called time, and everyone but Chris and I seemed to move with quickness. They scurried; we clung to the moment. Chris manipulated the cuffs to press his left hand to the glass, and I met it with my right. He looked me straight in the eyes and said, "I love you, sis. I miss y'all so much. I'll call you later. Answer the phone!" My mind wandered briefly to the bills I'd paid for these expensive phone calls. "Of course," I told him emphatically, "I'll be waiting, and I love you, too." Then came that familiar, agonizingly sad stare. I wanted to cry, but not in front of him. I swallowed hard, headed to the elevator to leave, and let it rip for the ride three floors down.

Earlier that spring, Chris had discovered in his cell a gift from a previous occupant: a tiny hole in the frosted window that overlooks a main street, a parking lot, and a visitors' walkway. As we left the building, I was so focused on finding the microscopic crack, that I crossed Jelani's path and lost my footing. He caught me, thank God, and held my hand as our gingerly stroll turned into a near crawl. Drumbeats resounded from all over; other invisible men were watching, communicating with us, too. And then I heard my brother, "I love you, Crys! Love you, Bro!" We smiled and yelled back, "We love you!" At the gate, a guard IDed us again, and with a bogus accent and a glint of sarcasm, said, "Okay, folks, y'all come back real soon." I ignored the jerk. Jelani looked at his watch. It was a quarter to 6:00. By the County's naive standards, we'd had a nice long visit.

★   ★   ★

I haven't been back in over a year, though if Chris hadn't posted bail, I would have had no choice but to oblige the fake Southern belle. Luckily for both my brother and me, a communal purse was on his side. The state's attorney, however, was not. During the bond hearing, that zealot paced the bench, spinning fact and fiction so persuasively that even I didn't recognize the caricature he'd made of Chris. Then came the big finish: a stunning request to hold my brother on a whopping million-dollar bail. Chris himself has never had much more than two pennies to rub together. And although, as a family, we live comfortably with almost as much of what we want as what we need, money doesn't grow on trees. Excuse my parents for not having the forethought to build a war chest for their kids' legal troubles alongside our college funds. A million dollars, really? My blood is boiling now, just thinking about it. Before I go too far down that road, I should remind myself that the proposal was nothing personal; the attorney was simply doing his job. He didn't know Chris from a can of paint, or more appropriately, from the drag of other brothers who ambled in and out of the courtroom that day. To him, Chris was a manila folder, measured in worth by whatever some clerk had stuffed into it.

Nobody familiar with the basics of bargaining would be amazed to learn that the highball offer of the state's attorney gave the judge permission to meet him halfway, at $500,000. After the hearing, my mother went to work—draining bank accounts, charging cards, and calling in outstanding favors. Meanwhile, my stepdad and Chris' dad, Roy, refused to spare another dime, and threatened to leave Mom if she did. Looking at the pattern of their son's young life, Roy had asked, what's it going to be—him or me? Ultimatums are poisonous seeds that take root, spreading far and wide into tangled webs of cynicism, hurt, and resentment. My stepdad's ultimatum germinated in Mom for 9 months before she raised enough to get Chris out of jail. By then, Mom was over being forced to choose sides; she ponied up the dough and made peace with the fact that her husband would do whatever he needed to do—divorce notwithstanding. I won't say much more about their marital affairs, except that I'm glad my stepdad stayed. The point is that a mother is only as happy as her unhappiest child, and mine put everything on the line to bring hers home.

Actually, Chris didn't come straight back to my parents' house. He made a pit stop at mine. Chris moved in with me, Jelani, and our two boys to get out of his dad's way. It was a temporary arrangement, but I picked up most of what I know about the person Chris is today during the 3 weeks we lived under the same roof. Let me run down what I observed: Chris smokes cigarettes—Newports, I think—when he's bored and after meals. He bores easily and survives on a simple diet of ramen noodles, sugary cereal, potato chips, and cold-cut sandwiches. Chris won't let his cellphone out of his sight, and the second it jingles, he answers immediately and takes the chitchat outside. He is in recovery. I gave Chris a lift to rehab one night on the west side of the city, and he showed me, along the way, where he often scored the tobacco-weed-PCP mix that had brought him to his knees. He is an insomniac, and though I figured my low-key lifestyle would lend itself to better sleep, he can't stand silence. As soft-spoken as Chris is, he likes noise—noisy people and things, and he's particularly attached to gadgets—blaring televisions and computers. On television, he prefers to watch scary movies, but every household has its rules and ours is strict about TV. On a computer, he only uses the Internet, and YouTube.com is by far his favorite site. Where else in the world are so many opportunists gathered where Chris, an inveterate songwriter, can share the lyrics he came up with while lounging in my basement?

It is late at night, and the kids are in bed. I am typing on a split screen—this essay is to the left and one of my brother's music videos is playing on the right. "We Got That," as it's been titled, is a collaboration between Tru Lou, Capo V (Chris), and Lil Mister. It opens with the three of them shoulder-to-shoulder in a tiny hotel bathroom, a bunch of dancing extras in the background—plastic cups in hand, joints ablaze, near-empty liquor bottles held high like winning prizes. My brother's ex-girlfriend, the video's eye candy, is half-naked, booty bouncing in an oversized tub to a hard beat and a catchy, bragging hook. Thirty seconds in, it's clear the song is an ode to the fast life—glamorizing guns, fashion, sex, money, and drugs—typical hip-hop posing.

When I saw the video for the first time, just before Chris moved out, I was shocked, though not for obvious reasons. Vulgarity, misogyny, and pretending aside, what surprised me in him was the resilience of a phoenix rising. Call me sentimental, but there is something to be said for the will to go from inmate to rap star in 3 weeks flat.

Chris is serious on the subject of music—always has been—but it wasn't until high school that he threw himself into making his own. When he reached the age of 16, my mother broke down and bought him the essentials of a functional recording studio: a laptop, a microphone and stand, a headset, and Fruity Loop production software for arranging his sounds and lyrics. He installed the equipment that night and fiddled with it constantly to get a slew of tracks out of his head, into his ears, under his flow, and up on the Web where, with any stroke of fortune, an industry executive may have discovered him.

No word yet from a record company. But it looks like "We Got That" has been viewed 267,071 times since it surfaced, and I'm begging the cosmos that the state's attorney didn't help the tally. I realize now that I have heard Chris' verse, but I've never actually listened to it. The whole verse plays right into the most demonizing narratives surrounding African American boys and men, but it's the last line that really gets me. Was it defiance or plain old stupidity that led Chris to mention robbery? Either way, given the charges against him for armed robberies that he denies committing, I wish he had resisted the temptation of artistic liberty.

There are other videos in which Chris made a cameo after he had settled back home with my parents; they are Tru Lou's, and Chris is his sober, bopping, lip-synching hype man. The last of these videos was uploaded 8 months ago, around the day when, in an ironic twist of fate, Tru Lou turned himself in for a 5-year prison sentence and Chris attended his first college class.

At 20, Chris began his freshman year at an Illinois state university behind the curve. But he also had a solid cheering squad. My mother, who walked him through each step of the application process, handled the logistics—everything from organizing his course schedule and meeting each of his teachers, to scouting out quiet places on campus where Chris could study and selecting linens for the dorm room he'd share. I gave Chris my two cents on how to establish healthy relationships with his professors, at least as I have seen it done as a professor myself. Our cousin, who is close to Chris' age, works in Student Affairs helping nontraditional students transition to college and brought the best of her day job to bear on Chris. Among the three of us, and many other people back home wishing Chris well, we genuinely thought he had a chance.

Cheering, of course, cannot make up for inadequate academic preparation, and as quiet as it was kept, well wishes certainly wouldn't erase the looming threat of my brother's impending legal battles.

As far as I know, Chris confided the weight of his baggage to two people: his roommate and a girl he'd been seeing. Unlike Capo V, my brother's rap persona, Chris is not a womanizer. In fact, he's had only three girlfriends in his lifetime, and by his own admission, the ladies who pique his interest also make him feel a little awkward. He told me a story a few weeks ago about running into the younger sister of his childhood friend and, being floored to see her as a gorgeous, fully hatched woman, blowing the perfect opportunity she'd created for him to ask her out. "She was bad!" he said to me, which, in this instance, meant "good." "I just didn't know what to say." Away at college, it was more of the same. Chris wanted to get involved with someone who was beautiful and smart, but he felt divided—at once undeserving of a good girl yet as entitled to love and happiness as anyone else—while at the same time well aware of the precariousness of his situation.

All in all, I don't recall hearing much about his brief college experience. I know he followed the natural ebb and flow that most of us in higher education experience in a semester: beginning on a confident high note, growing anxious when the thrill is gone, careening through midterms with a hope and a prayer, and sprinting desperately toward the end. In the meantime, he maintained a discipline of the desk that enabled him to party most weekends guilt-free. He went to the school's basketball games, and to my chagrin, he found the fraternity scene unimpressive. He made acquaintances—some through a distant relative who was also a student at the same school—but he was too guarded to befriend. Mostly, Chris hung out with his roommate, though as roommates do, the guy sometimes got under my brother's skin.

On the last day of the term, the two of them were not speaking. They had gotten into a fight over a T-shirt, each swearing up and down that it belonged to him. The roommate walked away with the T-shirt, and in exchange, Chris must have reasoned, he would not miss a pair of jeans. Chris packed the roommate's pants along with his own belongings, returned his key to the student housing office, and waited at a buddy's place for a ride back to Chicago. A small thing got bigger. When his roommate couldn't find his jeans, he called the police to report them stolen. The cops ran my brother's name, arrested him on the spot, and charged him with felony residential burglary. "At my own house?" he had asked incredulously. Mom bailed him out a week later and the inflated charges have since been lowered to misdemeanor theft, but the kicker is that getting arrested for any reason violates the conditions of bond in Cook County. As soon as the state attorney's office finds out Chris caught a sixth case, any day now, he'll lose the bond and a warrant will be issued. That is a foregone conclusion. Ready or not, my brother is going back through the revolving door.

CHAPTER 2

School-to-Prison Pipeline

I T STRIKES A SPECIAL CHORD in me every time I meet some-one—someone in the field of education, especially—who has never heard of the school-to-prison pipeline. Ask a teacher or principal about it, and expect little more than a polite nod and smart use of context clues. No offense, but I've gotten that "I don't know what you're talking about, but something tells me I should" response more than a few times. I assume the problem is one of semantics. The term is not exactly part of everyday lingo, and across activist circles the mind-blowing idea that kids get funneled from systems of education to systems of criminal justice has been captured by a number of other nifty metaphors. I can think of three.

METAPHOR ONE:
SCHOOLHOUSE-TO-JAILHOUSE TRACK

A close cousin to the language that I use is *schoolhouse-to-jailhouse track*. Both phrases highlight the fact that my profession is hardly the great equalizer it's hyped up to be. But the phrase *schoolhouse-to-jailhouse track* points to something specific: It can be traced to work done by lawyers at the Advancement Project, a civil rights organization, who wanted to name the on-the-ground realities of "zero-tolerance." By now, zero-tolerance in our schools and workplaces is as common as dirt, but most 1980s babies are too young to remember how things got this way; I know I can't. The spike of juvenile homicides, the resulting public panic, the racially coded media frenzy around teenage "superpredators," and the passage of federal and state laws to mete them out—somehow, it all went over my head. To tell the truth, I was well into my doctoral studies when I caught up on this bit of U.S. history. And for a long while after, I carried a heavy stack of books and reports around in my catchall backpack, whipping them out like Bibles when I needed direction.

One spring semester I taught a class on urban educational policy, and the topic of "bad kids" emerged as a particular favorite among my students. Most everyone wanted to know how to run a tight ship, stay sane, and keep safe with so many "troublemakers" and "class clowns" in contemporary public schools. Whenever I pushed people to unpack the beliefs embedded within this kind of philosophy and everyday language, things always got ugly. Public schools were equated with city schools, and city kids with cultural poverty and dysfunction. The stock stories commodified by the mainstream media—the news, Hollywood films, cable network television, and the music industry—about pathological and dangerous youth poured. And the grapevine, with its salacious tales from the field, was cited as proof positive that some children—mostly poor kids and kids of color—will inevitably fall through the cracks.

As lively as these discussions were, **no one ever seemed to want to talk about the connections between how we think and talk about children and how we treat them in social and academic contexts.** A hush usually fell over the crowd when I suggested that demonizing ideology and discourse enables a whole web of relationships, conditions, and social processes—a social ecology of discipline—which works on and through the youth who rub against our understanding of "good" students. Part of my students' silence was certainly rooted in the fact that challenging and unlearning what we assume we know is uncomfortable, and that finagling around contradictions and tensions is easier than diving into and grappling with them. But I discovered that profound ignorance also accounted for the group of 25 future teachers' resistance to a deeper examination of the conversation around "bad kids." Herein lay the teachable moment that I seized by reaching into my bag.

The schoolhouse-to-jailhouse track conjures a vivid, evocative, and unambiguous image: poor and Black and Brown children being derailed from academic and vocational paths, and directed toward jails and prisons. Each year, as Civic Enterprises, a public policy firm, reported in *The Silent Epidemic* (2006), almost one-third of all public school students and nearly one-half of all youth of color do not graduate high school with their class. The problem is particularly acute for African Americans, who represent about 15% of those below the age of 18, but make up 14% of all school dropouts, 26% of all the youths arrested, 46% of those detained in juvenile jails, and 58% of all juveniles sent to adult prisons (Coalition for Juvenile Justice, 2006). This is not an ideological claim; the numbers speak for themselves.

Whole bodies of scholarship convey the magnitude of the plight facing Black adolescents, especially males, in our public schools. At all levels of the K–12 school trajectory—elementary, middle, and high— Black boys lag behind their peers academically. On every indicator associated with progress and achievement—enrollment in gifted programs, Advanced Placement classes, and otherwise enriched courses— Black males are vastly underrepresented. Conversely, in every category associated with failure and distress—discipline referrals, grade retention, and dropout rates—Black males are overrepresented (Noguera, 2008; Schott Foundation, 2004, 2010). Black boys have the lowest graduation rates in most states; nearly half of all Black adolescent males in the United States quit high school before earning a diploma.

My teacher education students sat up a little straighter when I told them about my brother's schooling experiences. Eyebrows rose when I pointed to the published material about the ways in which contemporary educational policies and practices—such as school punishment and the application of special education categories— work together to move young people like him from schools to jails.

School Punishment

It surprised them to learn that in 1994 federal legislation mandated a 1-year expulsion for any public school student in possession of a firearm on school grounds (Advancement Project, 2005). Shortly thereafter, the Safe School Act revised and broadened the law to prohibit any student from bringing a "dangerous weapon"—just about anything that looks harmful—to school. Predictably, the number of school expulsions exploded, and disproportionately affected Black youth.

Zero Tolerance: Resisting the Drive for Punishment in Schools (Ayers, Dohrn, & Ayers, 2001), a book that I assigned to the class, was written in response to this reality. Contributing authors to the edited volume examine the dangers of zero-tolerance policies and explore alternatives; they tell stories from the ground floor of schools and classrooms; they examine the legal precedents that zero-tolerance policies bring in; they look at how the media enable and promote zero-tolerance, and what it means for students with disabilities; they deal with broad issues of race and racism in education, and the political economy that supports zero-tolerance; and they provide the statistical landscape of the problem. In the closing chapter, Michelle Fine and Kersha Smith (2001) synthesize the research to assess the impact of zero-tolerance policies, given their intended purposes and "unintended" consequences. They argue, in a succinct and concise way, that zero-tolerance policies are neither effective nor worth their salt, that they are neither equitable nor educational. Fine and Smith note, **"They do not make schools safer; they produce perverse consequences for academics, school/community relations, and the development of citizens; they dramatically and disproportionately target youth of color; and they inhibit educational opportunities"** (p. 260).

In response to a flurry of books and reports by academics, organizers, and journalists that effectively show how zero-tolerance punishes select students by depriving them of an education, some school districts have scrapped these policies. In Chicago, where I live and work, zero-tolerance policies in the district's schools were abolished in 2006 in favor of restorative justice approaches to harm and healing, but the number of suspensions has nearly doubled since then. Black boys in my hometown are five times more likely to be suspended than any other group of students in the city's public school system (Catalyst Chicago, 2009). Black boys comprise 23% of the district's student population, but amount to 44% of those who are suspended, and 61% of those who are expelled. One in four Black boys was suspended at least once in 2008. Black boys are the only group of Chicago Public School students whose suspension rates are higher in elementary school than in high school. In suburban Cook County, where my brother went to school, the racial disparity is also apparent: Black boys accounted for just 11% of students, but made up 35% of those suspended at least once and 44% of those expelled. At mixed-race schools, where Black male students comprise just 12% of enrollment, they make up 30% of those suspended and 54% of those expelled. The risk is great even at all-Black and predominantly Black schools, where the overall rate of suspensions and expulsions is highest.

The problem is much bigger than Chicago, however. Black youth, particularly males, are more likely than any other group in the United States to be punished in schools, typically through some form of exclusion. Black students are disciplined more frequently and harshly than their peers for less serious and more subjective reasons, such as disrespect, disruption, excessive noise, threats, and loitering, among others (Skiba, 2001). As unbelievable as the overdisciplining of Black students may seem to well-intentioned adults, it is all too real for the youth who experience it. Young people are sharp and extraordinarily attentive to their own thinking and the thinking of others. They know intuitively what we have spent more than 30 years documenting; they are well aware of these disciplinary discrepancies (Ferguson, 2001; Vavrus & Cole, 2002).

Rosa Hernandez Sheets (1996) reported that most students in an urban high school where she researched believed that race and racism were critical to the application of discipline. Although White students and teachers perceived racial disparity in discipline as being unintentional and unconscious, students of color saw it as conscious and deliberate, arguing that teachers often apply classroom rules and guidelines arbitrarily to exercise control or to remove students whom they do not like. In particular, Black students felt that a lack of respect, differences in communication styles, disinterest on the part of teachers, and purposeful marginalization were the primary causes of many disciplinary moments.

More than 10 years ago (2001), Ann Ferguson conducted a study of Rosa Parks Elementary School on the West Coast—where Black boys made up one-quarter of the student body, but accounted for nearly half the number of students referred for discipline; where three-quarters of those suspended were boys, and four-fifths of those were Black; and where Black males as young as 10 and 11 were routinely described as "at-risk" of failing, "unsalvageable," or "bound for jail." She tried to understand empirically what my class was engaging in theoretically: how school labeling practices and the exercise of rules worked as part of a hidden curriculum to marginalize and isolate Black boys in disciplinary spaces and brand them as criminally inclined. To explore these processes, Ferguson paid attention to everyday life at the school, observing all the sites to which she was given access and talking to kids and adults about their beliefs, relationships, and the common practices that give rise to a pattern in which the children who are sent to disciplinary spaces in school systems all across the United States are disproportionately Black and male.

In *Bad Boys: Public Schools in the Making of Black Masculinity* (Ferguson, 2001), another text on our reading list, Ferguson described what she found. Peering through a critical perspective, which presumes that schooling is a system for sorting and ranking students to take a particular place in the existing social hierarchy, Ferguson saw that the politics of "misbehavior" played out in the labeling of Black students as substandard or deficient and in the application of school rules. She learned that what counts as "proper" behavior was filtered through stereotypical representations, beliefs, and expectations that school adults held about their children. Black boys, in particular, were refracted through cultural images of Black males as both dangerous and endangered, and their transgressions were framed as different from those of other children. Black boys were doubly displaced. As Black children, they were not seen as childlike, but "adultified"; their misdeeds were "made to take on a sinister, intentional, fully conscious tone that is stripped of any element of childish naivete" (p. 83). As Black males, they were denied the masculine dispensation constituting White males as being "naturally naughty"; they were discerned as willfully bad (p. 80).

Perhaps Ferguson's greatest insight was that the youth themselves were acutely "aware not only of the institution's ranking and labeling system, but of their own and other children's position within that system" (p. 97), a perceptivity that shaped some of the boys' processes of disengaging from school.

The research is clear: Those who are absent from school—physically or mentally—perform poorly and are at risk of dropping out. A report published by the Civil Rights Project, a university-based think tank, notes that:

> Suspension is a moderate to strong predictor of a student dropping out of school; more than 30% of sophomores who drop out have been suspended. Beyond dropping out, children shut out from the education system are more likely to engage in conduct detrimental to the safety of their families and communities. (Civil Rights Project, 2000, p. 13)

Excessive discipline is often a critical first step out of schools for select youth—Black boys, in this case—who disproportionately find themselves in prison.

Special Education Categories

Being labeled as "disabled" nudges the other foot out of the schoolhouse door. We've known for decades that Black kids, especially young Black males, end up in subjective disability categories more often than other children. Critiques of the disproportional placement of Black youth in special education began circulating—at least among academics—as early as the 1960s, when people began to notice that schools had devised new ways to subvert the Supreme Court's 1954 desegregation decree (Dunn, 1968; Ferri & Connor, 2006). The story of the over-representation of youth of color in special education is a familiar one, but the numbers are no less unsettling. Black children constitute about 17% of all students enrolled in school, but they account for 33% of those identified as cognitively disabled. Black students are nearly twice as likely to be labeled "learning disabled" as White students, almost twice as likely to be labeled "emotionally disturbed," and three to four times as likely to be labeled "mentally retarded." Among all disability categories, mental retardation is the most likely to be assigned to Black youth, particularly Black males (Losen & Orfield, 2002; Parrish, 2002). Contrary to the expected trend, Black boys who attend school in wealthier communities are actually *more* likely to be labeled mentally retarded than those attending predominantly Black, low-income schools (Oswald, Coutinho, & Best, 2002).

The implications for Black youth of these three classifications in particular—Learning Disability (LD), Emotional Disturbance (ED), and Mental Retardation (MR)—are far-reaching. Students labeled ED and MR have the lowest graduation rates and the highest dropout rates (Hehir, 2005). More than half of all Black students with emotional and behavior problems leave school, and the majority of all students with emotional and behavior problems who do not finish high school are arrested within 3 to 5 years of dropping out (McNally, 2003). Young people without a high school diploma are more likely to be unemployed and underemployed, to earn less when they get a job than those with a high school diploma, and to be incarcerated (Petit & Western, 2004).

The data are consistent and robust, and many smart people agree that disagreement about the interpretation and application of these "judgment" categories is part of the problem. "Neither 'rationality' nor 'science'" control the process by which a child is assessed for these disabilities and referred for special education, Beth Harry and Janette Klingner (2005) wrote in their book, *Why Are So Many Minority Students in Special Education?* (p. 103). Rather, Harry and Klingner noted **six perspective-based factors that shaped the outcomes of conferences on eligibility and placement: (1) school personnel's impressions of the family, (2) a focus on intrinsic deficit rather than classroom ecology, (3) teachers' informal diagnoses, (4) dilemmas of disability definitions and criteria, (5) psychologists' philosophical positions, and (6) pressure from high-stakes testing to place a student in special education** (p. 103). The meaning of each "judgment" category has been understood differently across states, applied inconsistently within schools and districts, and shifted over time. As the category of MR became overpopulated with Black students in the early years after *Brown v.*

Board of Education, the new label of LD gave well-resourced families of White children a different and purportedly less stigmatizing way to explain their children's difficulties, to gain access to special services, and to set apart their children's disabilities from those of their peers of color (Ferri & Connor, 2006). With increasing legal pressure during the 1970s and throughout the 1980s to minimize the number of youth of color diagnosed as mentally retarded, the same effects of racial bias that had once produced high rates of mental retardation among this group were expressed instead through LD diagnoses (Ong-Dean, 2009). This contextualizes Harry and Klingner's (2005) report that the number of students labeled MR between 1974 and 1998 declined from 1.58% to 1.37% while those labeled ED increased from 1% to more than 5% and those labeled LD increased from 1.21% to 6.02% (p. 4).

Certainly, some students do benefit from the resources and accommodations that a disability label provides, but research shows that many do not (Fuchs & Fuchs, 1995; Slavin, 1989). More specifically, it suggests that special education is often a dumping ground for youth of color, and that Black boys are especially susceptible to being undereducated—labeled, shunned, and treated in ways that create and reinforce a cycle of failure.

When my students were sufficiently inundated with material, they urged me to help them sift through it and make sense of it all. I broke it down like this: **What I gather from some of the literature on zero-tolerance, school discipline, and special education is that these policies are panoptic systems of surveillance, exercises of power used to continuously and purposefully monitor poor youth and youth of color** (Foucault, 1977/1995). Black boys in particular are unevenly punished and tracked into educational disability categories in their early years, practices that tend to reinforce the very problems they are intended to correct. And although this is enough to make reasonable people want to holler, even more insidious is when those under surveillance internalize the experiences and labels assigned to them, when they believe the exclusion and isolation has been defensible, and when they learn to condition themselves. Then, Black boys who have been sorted, contained, and then pushed out of schools become

Black men—men whose patterns of hardship are pronounced and deeply entrenched; men who constitute nearly 50% of the adult males in prison; men who have been well primed for neither college, career, nor full participation in our democracy, but instead for punitive institutionalization.

I shudder as I write this. I am reminded that once upon a time, I was as sure as the sky is blue of how my brother got into such a mess—I was so sure that even Chris himself couldn't tell me otherwise. About 3 months after Chris dropped out of high school, I recall leading him to explain, while sitting at a bistro table in a café, what it was about school that made him want to leave, what repeated suspensions and a special needs label had to do with it, and what a miserable, dream-crushing existence the experience had created. I pressed him to mime the perfectly sensible explanations that scholars had given to me. But this is Chris I'm talking about. My brother's will is as strong as mine, and he said everything but "woe is me." "I can't blame it on nobody else" is the story he stuck to. I believed that Chris was being modest.

Today is not once upon a time, though, and in the span of the years since that spring semester, I've become less confident that I have Chris figured out. Not that the schoolhouse-to-jailhouse track doesn't speak to my brother's reality, but I am more open now to the fact that it isn't the whole truth and nothing but the truth.

According to Chris, the problem all started back in his freshman year, which he reconstructed for me a few years ago with the kind of clarity that one can only have in hindsight. On one April morning, Chris said, he sat in the last desk of the farthest row from his English teacher, looking down at a notebook cradled in his arm. He silently read the words "Chris Lord" and grinned, tickled at the flair he had given the name by layering a Southern drawl atop of his distinctly Midwestern accent. "Chris *Laud*." Chris had been doodling throughout the first block of his classes that seemed to drone on nonstop. Even when the teacher was conspicuously swaying toward him, rattling on about plot structure, sequence of events, and climax, Chris carefully added a cluster of stars and half-moons in chunky font to perfect the full page.

Chris was 14 and impressionable, though immune to the authority of most adults at the school. The 9th-grade English teacher, with her uncanny ability to deaden the one subject that Chris felt wholly capable of mastering, was by far his least favorite. Chris found it odd that he had been under her tutelage for months and yet she was still clueless about what made him tick. For instance, she had no idea that he thinks like an artist; original lyrics filled the bite-sized memory card of the cellphone she often threatened to take. And instead of tapping into his penchant for literary expression through song, rhythm, and rhyme, she triggered in him the stress of pure boredom that always ended badly. He fidgeted in his chair, took more trips to the wastebasket than necessary, talked, and talked back with impunity. He was also in the habit of escaping, as he had that morning, to the peace of his own mind, where he'd stay until the punishments of class had ceased. Occasionally he'd skip school altogether, which at that moment, he wished he'd considered much sooner.

But then there was the Blessing, a highly anticipated initiation, to mull over. Chris learned the day before that the Blessing would be planned, and here he was, imagining the celebrity attached to his new name with less than 4 hours until the school day was done, and contemplating missing the Blessing? Absolutely not.

The teacher hovered over his shoulder—arms crossed, brow raised—but rather than fight or flee, suddenly Chris went still, clutching his pad and pencil in midair, moving only his heavy eyes to meet hers blankly. They had a captive audience. All 20-plus kids in his class were watching intently, following the length of the teacher's neck as it first stretched to study Chris' drawing and then straightened in exaggerated emphasis.

"The climax," she declared, according to my brother, "is the highest point of a story, surrounded by rising and falling action." She surveyed the room and let her glare fall firmly on Chris. "For the character, it marks a change for the better," she said, unfolding each of her hands and bobbing in synch, "or for the worse." Chris detested the public shaming, but wasted few moments with anger, or humiliation, or wondering why the teacher did not simply call him out, write him up, and send him packing to the Dean's office, again.

He emptied the warm air in his chest and thanked God, giving gratitude to a power that he neither knows well nor frequently summons, but that somehow came through for him in the nick of time.

A bell rang. Chris remembered rushing through the massive outpouring of classes, down three flights of stairs, and into the cafeteria, scanning the string of tables for a crowd surrounding Geronimo. At 17—3 years older than Chris—Geronimo was the quintessential cool kid, appealing to pockets of students in the school's labyrinth of a social scene—the jocks, the potheads, the geeks, the thespians, the thugs, and the ghosts who, in a cruel teen spirit, some pretended not to see. Geronimo commanded respect; with a paternal confidence, he was equally adept at throwing his weight around his peers and charming the pants off the skeptics among them. With similar finesse, Geronimo wooed Chris and a flock of nine boys lingering over lunch, rehearsing details and doling out responsibilities to be executed to the letter. Chris, eager to please, committed his part to memory.

It was during English one day the previous semester that Chris had retreated to a remote bathroom in the building's E Wing, and, upon opening the door, detected the familiar potpourri of tobacco and weed ablaze. He peeked around the corridor and followed the scent to the sink, where a young man was perched with silky smoke roaming overhead. Chris had seen the man around and knew him to be older from his fuzzy mustache.

Chris was about to turn to leave when the man asked, "What's up, little homey?" flicking his chin at Chris. Chris paused for a moment to consider its meaning. In American lingo, the phrase "What's up?" is nothing but a casual greeting, often spouted in passing with no expectation or pause for a response. In Chris' world, "what's up?" is a complicated code that must be ciphered exactly as it was intended, though no one, including Chris, knows of a foolproof way to do so. Yet he has never confused, let's say, a challenge to battle with a proposition for sex, or mistook a blithe compliment for a bridge to sustained conversation. And so when the man addressed him while wearing a rogue smile, Chris safely assumed that he just meant he could use some company.

"What you doing over here?" the man inquired, extending to Chris what remained of a slim joint. Though school security guards rarely canvassed the E Wing, where special needs students were contained, he glanced over his shoulders before accepting the offer.

"Nothing. Just chilling," Chris explained. "Just trying to get away."

Chris hiked up his drooping pants and leaned against a cool basin to the side of him. The two of them shared a brief silence until the man broke in, admitting that he was a recent transplant from the city's far south side, which apart from its geography, existed as an expression of Chris' imagination. From television news, neighborhood tales, and his own periodic observations, Chris had gathered that the city was entrenched with crime, drugs, and violence; city kids were both dangerous and exotic. To Chris, this man—big, Black, and bold—was emblematic of this narrative, which is why his generosity and ease threw Chris for a loop. Chris tossed out the names of the few city blocks that he could remember, hoping for credibility and commonality upon which to build. The man grew up in the hood. With hesitance, Chris spoke of his background, all of it lived with our family in suburbs that were considerably less hectic than the city's core. Chris was asked whether he belonged to one of the two street gangs that dominated the school's student body, a question that Chris had prepared himself to answer wryly. "I'm a Vice Lord," Chris said, having deliberately chosen the least populated group, to lessen the likelihood that he'd be forced to admit he couldn't prove it. Lucky for Chris, the man needed no evidence. By the time Chris heard soles squeaking in the hall, he did not know how many minutes he and the young man had gone on talking about recreational drug use and favorite pastimes and rap music and girls and clothes. But within seconds, Chris had straightened his pearly white T-shirt, nodded to the man, and headed back to class, the door swinging shut behind him.

It was only through the grapevine that Chris learned that he had just met Geronimo, who had single-handedly organized some 40-odd teenagers into a clique that was well known, ironically, as the Wild Foes. One week later, Chris formally introduced himself to Geronimo, and 2 weeks after that he was fist-pumped and high-fived by most of the motley crew Geronimo had managed to band together peacefully. Chris was hooked, and for months he negotiated the tension of bearing witness to and often participating in the group's daily grind without permission to claim the Wild Foes as his own people. But now, finally, happy with Chris' salesmanship, they were breaking bread and going over the particulars of his last moments as a wannabe.

At the designated hour, Chris told me, the Wild Foes met discreetly behind a sandwich shop close to the school's campus, which they had gerrymandered to cut off opposing squads. Encircling Geronimo, the boys assumed a pose beyond their years—shoulders stout, hands over clenched fists, legs widespread—like men on security detail.

From his backpack, Geronimo extracted a worn copy of the Holy Quran and leafed to a page that had been marked by a folded sheet of spiraled notepad paper. He unfolded the note, reviewed its contents, and tucked it neatly into the pocket of his leather jacket. With the rise of Geronimo's palms, Chris first saw every eye shut and every head bow like clockwork, and then he reluctantly followed suit.

"In the name of Allah," Geronimo began, "most gracious and most merciful." The boys joined in the tongue twister: "Praise be to Allah the cherisher and sustainer of the worlds; most gracious, most merciful; master of the Day of Judgment. Thee do we worship, and thine aid we seek. Show us the straightway, the way of those whom hast bestowed thy grace, those whose portion is not wrath, and who go not astray." Though Chris did not understand most of the prayer that he regurgitated on cue, his stomach fluttered, and he bellowed a big "Amen!"

Geronimo noticed, and called his enthusiastic recruit toward the circle's center. Why, he asked Chris, do you want to join the Wild Foes? Wilting under the weight of Geronimo's arm, Chris eked out a hackneyed spiel about loyalty, girls, and big fun.

"For you, my brother," Geronimo concluded, "I give my unity and vitality. I give you my undying love. Almighty!" And just like that, with Geronimo's simple Blessing, Chris Smith became Chris Lord. Later on, at the neophyte party, Chris lost himself in vodka until he grew sick, then hobbled three blocks from home to vomit someplace where the family would not see.

At half past 8:00 the next morning, Chris dragged himself onto his feet, dizzy, knees limp. Chris awoke with the feeling that yesterday's pain was the next day's gain, having come to a crossroads, a space of belonging and authenticity where he hoped to achieve some realistic power over the world within which he lived. After a half-mile schlep to school, Chris dozed through classes and cheered up between them; he walked the hall knowing that word of his initiation had spread across campus. At lunchtime, Chris made his way to the cafeteria where he mingled and schmoozed with his brethren all around. Geronimo was the only one missing. Along with Chris' place at the table came the disappointing news that Geronimo had to report for a stint in in-house suspension. So instead of parleying with the group's leader, Chris sat opposite Doug E., Geronimo's longtime sidekick and substitute, exchanging cryptic monosyllables.

"I like that phone," Doug E. said, pointing to a boy eating alone two tables over with a razor-thin mobile phone on his tray.

"Yeah?" Chris glanced behind him, indifferent. He planned an exit strategy, peeked over and around, sizing up each of four lunch lines.

"I like that phone," Doug E. said again, straight-faced and vigilant.

Back and forth they went like this until Chris finally got the drift. "Come on," Chris said, swatting the shoulder of a lurking recruit who would do whatever he was told. "Let's get it."

Chris and the recruit, both little more than 5 feet tall and skinny, confronted the phone's owner. "Hey, my man over here likes that phone," Chris said. "As a matter of fact, I think that *is* his phone," he said, curling his fingers into tight balls.

"Fuck out of here, dude," the other student responded, shooing Chris off.

At first, Chris was more perplexed than moved by the boy's firm dismissal and the speed with which he offered it, taking no more than a nanosecond to see right through the Chris' smoke screen. Chris turned to the recruit, who looked to Doug E., who was observing every move; all were stuck briefly in a struggle of wills, gauging their own performance under bright lights.

And then Chris lunged. He wrapped his arms around the boy's neck, demanding that he give it up! The boy squirmed, wriggled a way out of the head lock, and then he was upon Chris. The recruit stepped in with a sucker punch to the boy's temple. The boy passed out in Chris' hands, flaccid, like a surprise trust fall caught out of obligation. Chris threw the boy to the floor, kicked him for a grand finish, and walked away with neither the phone nor the faintest idea that from here everything would slide downhill.

I don't know how any of this foolishness went unnoticed by my family, as nosy and tight-knit as we are. My people are strict and they have some old-fashioned sensibilities, especially about childrearing. I will never forget my last bare-bottomed whooping: I was 11 going on 21, pubescent, and mortified to receive the most coordinated thrashing-lecture of my life for traipsing to a local Walgreens without my mother's permission. My mother had bad nerves and she didn't set curfews because the idea of my sister and I doing whatever with whomever until whenever was the equivalent, in her mind, of child neglect. Our every move was usually the calculated result of pre-meditated thought and intense negotiations. My mama did not play. Her mother was another force to be reckoned with. When we were younger, my parents, my sister, and I shared a house on the far south side of Chicago, with my mother's mom and dad. On our long city block, Grandma designated a neighbor's front yard about four houses down either side of ours as the wanderlust boundary, which she dared us to extend a tiptoe beyond. Chris doesn't believe me and my sister when we tell him that we couldn't cross the street without supervision or stay out after the streetlights had come on until our early teens. By then, Mom was in her mid-30s. She had divorced, remarried, moved our newly blended family to a quiet suburb, and birthed the last of her children and her only boy. That is to say, Mom's views had changed about a lot of things.

My mother ruled her girls with an iron fist, but Chris less so. She brought us up in a village of extended and fictive kin. My brother's significant others were his evolving roster of friends. Mom sent me and my sister to public schools with kids and adults who looked like us. Chris went private. Mom was a constant presence in our schools—helping out, establishing relationships, building capital. For Chris, she was constantly on the defense and putting out fires. I am suspicious of people who throw parents—especially mothers—under the bus when children act up. But it'd be dishonest if I said that I haven't considered the possibility that my mother raised her daughters and loved her son.

Despite these differences, my siblings and I belong to the same imperfect, adoring, loyal clan, and everybody in it would be utterly appalled to hear my brother's version of events. Naturally, we'd eventually turn our gaze inward and mine old memories for telltale signs that were somehow missed. If I've done my math correctly, all of this must have happened around 2007, the year that Grandma's cancer began to dictate family matters. What I remember about that period was being absorbed by the tension in our house, the daily grind of round-the-clock care, and the incessant fear of losing someone so instrumental to our lives. When she died, we were crushed.

To Grandma's funeral, Chris wore a monochromatic scheme of black—an oxford shirt, tailored slacks, and an unauthorized pair of designer shades—deliberately chosen to deflect the light of day. Chris wanted to go unnoticed. He wanted to pay his respects undisturbed, in quiet meditation, with a soulful rendition of the hymn "Going up to Yonder" as white noise. Between sips of hot chocolate, Chris explained why. He said that 4 days earlier, the Wild Foes bore down on someone with whom Geronimo claimed to have bad blood and Chris got mixed up in the fallout of retaliation: He was spotted at a local pizza parlor, followed as he left the restaurant alone, chased and clobbered to settle the score. Chris thought the aftermath looked monstrous. He had arrived home late from school, battered and trembling, relaying a half-baked story about random acts of violence. How could Chris begin to explain that he'd befriended gangsters, that the thrill of pretending to be one had been reason enough to join a group whose raison d'être was being bad, that he'd mindlessly carried out marching orders, that some poor guy had felt and avenged his wrath—who and why exactly, he did not really know? What would people think?

Chris said he pictured how the whole scene might have played itself out. His father, Roy, would have taken a hard line. He would have neither believed Chris nor bothered to get to the bottom of things; instead, he would offer Chris a few trash bags to collect the most essential of his belongings. Roy simply wouldn't have had it in him to investigate another of Chris' exploits, the third in as many months. School officials had settled the first. The law handled the second. And before these, there were 5 exhausting years of sporadic problems that nearly pushed Roy over the edge. His face glazed with oil after a 10-hour shift climbing poles for AT&T, Roy would have rested easily, gaze slight and heavy, on a stool at the breakfast bar across from me as I documented the unfolding drama. Chris imagined himself grinning and bearing my paying scrupulous attention to him, asking a gazillion questions, and scribbling illegible notes to later scrutinize and blow up beyond proportion. "It's just me," he would've said again and again. "Sis, this ain't got nothing to do with school." Andrea would have likely agreed and waxed philosophic over how our parents might have handled something like this back in our day. Mom would have blushed—while Roy surrendered, while I wrote, while Andrea reminisced—until she finally collapsed in agony.

These thoughts swirled in and out of Chris' mind as he was simultaneously nursed and grilled by the whole family fussing over him at the front door. But Chris wanted to say nothing more. He pulled away from the crowd and skipped every other step up to his bedroom, where he hid until the funeral. He was low-key in the congregation, surrounded by countless relatives who, in their own grief, neither doubted his fashion sense nor asked questions whose answers would only deepen the lies Chris had already told.

METAPHOR TWO:
CRADLE-TO-PRISON PIPELINE

Marian Wright Edelman and the advocates at the Children's Defense Fund did not trademark the "cradle-to-prison pipeline" in light of families like mine. Still, I can appreciate the utility in any framework that tries to help wrap my head around the predictors of incarceration. In a seminal report written for the Children's Defense Fund (2007), Edelman writes at length:

So many poor babies in rich America enter the world with multiple strikes already against them: without prenatal care and at low birth weight; born to a teen, poor and poorly educated single mother and absent father. At crucial points in their development, from birth through adulthood, more risks and disadvantages cumulate and converge that make a successful transition to productive adulthood significantly less likely and involvement in the criminal justice system significantly more likely.

Lack of access to health and mental health care; child abuse and neglect; lack of quality early childhood education to get ready for school; educational disadvantages resulting from failing schools that don't expect or help them achieve or detect and correct early problems that impede learning; zero tolerance school discipline policies and the arrest and criminalization of children at younger and younger ages for behaviors once handled by schools and community institutions; neighborhoods saturated with drugs and violence; a culture that glorifies excessive consumption, individualism, violence and triviality; rampant racial and economic disparities in child and youth serving systems; tougher sentencing guidelines; too few positive alternatives to the streets after school and in summer months; and too few positive role models and mentors in their homes, community, public and cultural life overwhelm and break apart fragile young lives with unbearable risks. (Children's Defense Fund, 2007, pp. 3–4)

This much I get. Some children are born on the path to prison. They aren't derailed from the right track; they haven't been given a fighting chance to get on it in the first place.

Of all the school-to-prison pipeline metaphors, the "cradle-to-prison pipeline" is probably the least off-putting for most people, after the visceral sensation of the imagery has passed. Personally, the phrase *cradle-to-prison pipeline* is too self-flagellating for my taste, too straight-shooting in its emphasis on everything that poor families don't have and will presumably never have or on what they do have but shouldn't. Not that sugar-coating the devastation of poverty will make it more palatable, but I can just see it now: all the neo–Bill Cosbys of the world, sashaying on their soapboxes armed with the "America's Cradle-to-Prison Pipeline" storyline, urging the poor—understood as the Black poor—to pull themselves up and "Come on, people." In fairness, I do realize that there are other layers to the metaphor, so I'll turn down the volume now—way down—on the bootstrap rhetoric to free up mental space where I can think about them.

If all I took from the term *cradle-to-prison pipeline* was permission to attack adults who make choices that create chaos for kids, then I'd be missing the point entirely. Beside the fact that choices are inextricably linked to power—the more or less power you have, the greater or fewer choices there are available—they are rarely decided upon in a vacuum. What the cradle-to-prison pipeline really tries to holistically critique is a broad range of structural conditions under which extraordinary family dysfunction and a route to nowhere makes logical sense. It rails against macroeconomic policies and practices like those that inadequately regulate preventative health care, quality education, affordable housing, and living wage work as flat-out wrong and gravely dangerous. As Edelman notes, "Without significant interventions by families, community elders and institutions, and policy and political leaders to prevent and remove these multiple, accumulated obstacles, so many poor and minority youths are and will remain trapped in a trajectory that leads to marginalized lives, imprisonment and premature death" (Children's Defense Fund, 2007, p. 4).

I am reminded of Michelle Alexander's convincing book *The New Jim Crow* (2012) about why mass incarceration—of more than 2 million people at last count—is another piece of this larger social order that is in need of altering. Alexander argues that, much like slavery and the Jim Crow laws of our not-so-distant past, mass incarceration functions as a sophisticated system to relegate Black folks to second-class citizenship. Here, in a nutshell, is how Alexander says the system works: First, the police stop, interrogate, search, and round up an unprecedented number of people, primarily poor men of color, for minor drug crimes. Second, defendants generally have weak legal representation and face strong pressure to plead guilty—which they often do—whether they are guilty or not, especially when prosecutors use their prerogative to pile on extra charges. Third, after spending a great deal of time under correctional supervision—in jail or prison, on probation or parole—the vast majority of convicted offenders are released back into their communities with little more than a bus ticket. Forget rebuilding lives; they will never be integrated into mainstream society. Alexander (2012) reminds us: "They will be discriminated against, legally, for the rest of their lives—denied employment, housing, education, and public benefits." Assisted by public consensus, White supremacy, and the criminal justice system, "most will eventually return to prison and then be released again, caught in a closed circuit of perpetual marginality" (p. 181).

METAPHOR THREE:
SCHOOL-PRISON NEXUS

I don't know what to do with myself when I read this kind of stuff, except maybe phone Chris, hug my sons a little tighter, and rush off to write or teach as though lives depend on it—all before resettling, eventually, in my cozy roost with some other disturbing manuscript to plow through. Not long before *The New Jim Crow*, it was my friend and colleague Erica Meiners' book *Right to Be Hostile* (2007) that rocked my world. The book unpacks what activists and scholars have referred to as the "prison industrial complex," or the politics and business of corrections, to which Meiners claims schools are parties. To build the case (which is persuasive from the get-go), she points out that some schools look and feel an awful lot like prisons. Meiners begins by describing the "schoolhouse-to-jailhouse track." She builds on the same contemporary research on school-based practices that I've already described and then widens the frame to show interconnections among education, incarceration, and other important forces. For example, she describes changes in the welfare state and other economic shifts over the past 3 decades, explaining mysteries like stagnation in education-related funding alongside ballooning resources for prisons and policing: Basically, the mainstream media, private companies, and poor rural communities tell us that we need them, and schools help fill them. Meiners riffs on the creation of sex offender registries to show how schools legitimate concepts, such as "the child," that require protection and expansion of the prison industrial complex. She addresses the construction and management of identities: "Just as our schools produce gifted children, successful learners, good kids, we simultaneously require and produce the inverse, remedial learners, educational failures, bad seeds, and more" (Meiners, 2007, p. 167). Meiners' book is hard going, but it helps me see that the conceptual and material movement of young people from schools to jails is neither neat nor direct. For these reasons, Meiners foregoes pathway metaphors altogether in favor of another one: "school-prison nexus."

There are several ways, then, to talk about the school-to-prison pipeline, each of which offers a rather different lens. The school-house-to-jailhouse track enables a heavy analysis of what is happening in schools, and what harmful policies and practices teachers, principals, and superintendents have some latitude to redress. The cradle-to-prison pipeline metaphor paints many systemic issues with broad strokes to highlight points of conflict and opportunity in family, community, and national priorities. The school-prison nexus pushes us to confront and debunk an even bigger system at work, and what it means for schools and schoolchildren. Not being so sure of myself, I tend to use the safest, most popular, and noncommittal wording in my own work, but name it what you will—so long as it is named.

CHAPTER 3

The Tipping Point

THE OTHER DAY, Chris was insistent: "Something's wrong with me, gotta be. I do stuff without thinking. I'm impulsive." I didn't disagree with his assessment; the possibility has crossed my mind more than a few times. Still, *impulsive* is an odd choice of words for my brother. *Reckless*, I'll go with. *Wild* sounds more like him. *Impulsive* is too textbook perfect.

The doctor's note reads, in part:

> Please be advised that I am the board certified psychiatrist who is currently treating Christopher Smith. . . .
>
> He was initially evaluated by this examiner on July 3, 2013, and diagnosed with Bipolar 2 Disorder, Generalized Anxiety Disorder, and Attention Deficit/Hyperactivity Disorder-Combined Type. As a result, this patient was prescribed Seroquel XR and titrated to a dose of 300 mg each night for treatment of Bipolar 2 Disorder.
>
> There has been some improvement on the medication. However, due to side effects, the dose of Seroquel XR will be decreased to 200 mg PO QHS. Once his mood is stabilized, he will be placed on medication for treatment of ADHD.

I can't imagine which is worst: a racing, manic mind; a mind-numbing depression; or a drug-induced stupor. But Chris has been openly struggling with all three in recent weeks. His acceptance that "something's wrong" is significant, by the way. When Chris was a teenager, he fought tooth and nail against the alphabet soup of illnesses and disabilities, as well as everything that having one of them might have said about him. Bipolar and anxiety disorder are news to me, but Chris was said to suffer from ADHD more than a decade ago. Why the sudden change of heart? One possibility is that after years without proper treatment, his condition is so out of hand that he has to take care of it, or else. Or it could be that he's meticulously crafting a paper trail to help strengthen his defense. Maybe both fit the bill. It is true, though, that Chris and everybody else on the planet is a universal receiver: we pick up language and ideas that, with repetition, tend to become the reality that we live.

THE DIFFERENCE A "DIFFERENCE" MAKES

My brother says his involvement with the wrong crowd did him in. I believe that; really, I do. Whenever I dig at how Chris got here, I also zoom back to the hormonal havoc and vulnerability of his adolescence, except my memory is shorter than my brother's; I get stuck in 2008, the year straight out of hell. It got off to an ominous start. Mom's father passed away, then her mother, and her cousin right after that—three funerals within the first few months of the year. Deep down, I thought that the old folks were mistaken about tragedy coming in threes, but in the midst of our third, I so desperately wanted to believe. At least I could have expected the sea of despair that had nearly swallowed the family whole to finally let up, but no, that wasn't happening just yet. All my hopes were dashed when, in the funk of a recession, Chris dropped out of high school, and I worried that forever he would be gone, too.

On the day he left school with pleasure, but without a diploma, basic necessities like food and gas were more expensive than they had been in the past, homes were less valuable, big spenders had turned frugal, and dignified jobs that paid living wages were hard to come by. I remember that moment especially because I was a broke doctoral student at the time, and I knew that even with an advanced degree, in a flooded market, my chances of finding a position were slim.

So the consideration of what a young Black man would do with few skills and no credentials scared me, and as commendable as it was for Chris to have a plan, his proposal didn't allay my fear. He would go to the Job Corps, of all places, the U.S. Department of Labor's boarding school for "the bottom of our society." Not my words, of course, I lifted them from another Chris—Chris Weeks, a political staffer who was on the ground floor of the Job Corps' origin back in the 1960s. Weeks (1967) wrote in *Job Corps: Dollars and Dropouts*: The program was "focused on a specific problem of undeniably critical proportions—masses of teenagers who had been born into and raised in poverty, and who, because of this background, had little hope for earning a decent income or becoming productive citizens during their lives"—a problem that had long been complicated by weak government efforts to help. "To solve this problem"—again, not my words—"it seemed to have a promising formula for success—take these youngsters out of their ghetto tenements and rural shacks and put them in a clean, healthful Job Corps center where massive injections of remedial education and job training would turn them into law-abiding, tax-paying good neighbors" (p. 5). Insulting, don't you think?

My brother had a different, benign, self-gratifying outlook on things. He was sold on the incentives that drew more than 300,000 applications from all across the country within 3 months of the program's inception and today pull in some 60,000 youth each year. In the Job Corps, Chris could get a GED, three square meals per day, spending money, help finding work, and a small stipend to hold him over until his first paycheck came. He'd have ample spare time for sports and recreation, could pick up a trade such as tile setting or carpentry, and could live away from home for the first time with people of his own age. I had my reservations about the idea, but I could understand the allure: Whatever his everyday life was like in high school paled in comparison to the sexiness of the Job Corps.

Chris told me something to that order in a soft whisper a month before he joined. We were sitting in the stuffy conference room of a community center with a few handfuls of other young people. Mom was waiting right outside. There were two window units that should have pushed cool air, nine tables, and fewer people than available chairs—more than enough space to accommodate all three of us—but we were late, and the woman who was facilitating the Job Corps admissions event was no-nonsense. She would only allow one of us to come along with Chris, and Mom insisted that it be me. Chris and I settled in the back next to three dark-skinned brothers who reeked of cigarettes and who were worried about whether they'd have to allow the Job Corps to complete a background check to apply. That wouldn't be necessary, the woman said. Recruits must be U.S. citizens, young, and poor—poor by whose standards, she didn't say.

We missed her formal presentation, but we had already been on the Job Corps' website; we knew the drill. This information session kicked off the first of four stages in the journey to complete the program. In the "Outreach and Admissions" stage, Chris would visit admissions counselors, gather information, and submit an application packet. Once admitted, he'd prepare and leave for one of 125 centers somewhere in the United States. The Job Corps could provide transportation to and from the center, but Chris wouldn't need it. Upon arrival, Chris would focus on adjusting to life at the center, as well as academic testing, health screening, and instruction on resume building, computer literacy, and job search skills in the Career Preparation Period. Within a month or so, he would enter the Career Development Period, in which he'd choose an academic path—a GED certificate or an online high school diploma—and a trade. He would receive academic instruction, vocational training, drivers' education, and prepare for a career and independent life outside of the Job Corps. After graduation, the Career Transition Period would start and specialists from Dynamic Educational Systems, Inc., a private company that has agreements with the Department of Labor and other employment training contractors, could assist him in securing a job, joining the military, or enrolling in some other training program, and with finding housing, transportation, and other support services.

"I might have some pull in St. Louis," the woman said as she handed out applications. "Humphrey, in Minnesota, won't take anyone from Chicago. They think y'all are trouble." The nearest centers, Chicago and Joliet, were not accepting males for at least a couple of months. "I know y'all can't wait that long," she said, "and I *know* parents don't want to."

Chris anxiously grabbed a pen and started working on the paperwork. "Don't you want to go sit with Mom and fill this out?" I asked.

"Naw, I'm not retarded," Chris said, but then he remembered that she'd been out there alone, and changed his mind.

Mom found several mistakes on his application and she tried to help him through them. He wrote his name, "Chris," and Mom insisted that he list his full given name instead, but when they got to the end of the application and he again signed "Chris," Mom was steaming. Her face tightened. Her voice deepened. She spoke in short, quick commands.

"Your name is not Chris," Mom said.

"Yes, it is," Chris told her.

"No, it's not," she insisted. "Write your name." When he didn't, she said, "Fuck it, we're leaving." She got up from the table and walked toward the door. I followed her.

Chris kept writing. "I'm staying to finish," he said.

"It's a game to him," Mom said, turning to me.

I tried to play the role of mediator. "Your application should probably match your Social Security card and birth certificate, both of which Mom brought with her," I said to Chris. I'm not sure if that was Mom's logic, but it seemed to do the trick. We were the last people to leave the session that afternoon, uptight and uncomfortable, and careful of the next step.

The three of us returned to the same place where we'd managed to avert a crisis a week earlier. We were scheduled to meet with an admissions counselor to pick up and go over additional application forms, but she explained that a demanding boss needed her and that she could not see us. Before leaving us in an empty hallway, she frantically handed over the paperwork, pointed to signature lines, made a few copies, and gave us directions to tuck his completed application packet under her office door.

We pulled a few worn chairs around a table and Mom began working on the papers. She came to a question about his medical history and disabilities, and she paused. She repeated and pondered the question. Should she reveal the disorder that she had been helped to see in Chris and that Chris refused to believe even exists?

"No! Say no," Chris urged.

Mom said nothing, but kept working. Reading Mom's decision, Chris grunted and smiled widely. She had obliged.

"Why you do that?" he asked, assuming that she had not kept the uncertain information between us simply because he'd asked.

"I don't want them to hold up your application," she said. "They can worry about that"—identifying and dealing with his unique learning needs—"when you get in."

She placed the paperwork in an envelope with seven short essays that Chris had written on his own. "I want them to see his true writing abilities," Mom told me. I wanted to see them, too, but Chris wouldn't let me.

Back in the car, Mom explained her plans to send Chris to the Joliet center near our home, but the gain of proximity to the familiar was matched by the loss of employable trades that were available to him right away. Beyond the union trades, such as carpentry and painting, that require candidates to be at least 17 years old, only vocations like business tech and facilities management were offered at Joliet. But because there is no such position as a "business tech" in the job market, Mom said, those weren't options for him. She was already drumming up ways to work through this conundrum at some opportune time in the future.

Chris was also looking ahead. "What you going to do when I graduate from Job Corps, Mama?" he asked.

"I'm going to throw a huge trunk party and buy outrageous gifts like Louis Vuitton sheets," Mom said, "if you take Job Corps seriously, learn to live on your own, and go on to college."

That same day, I gave Chris a lift to a barbershop near his high school. Along the way, I asked him what was going on there. He told me that he wasn't giving his teachers a hard time, but that he wasn't doing their assigned work, either. A progress report dated September 15 shows that he was on the way to four F's and a D in the sole chemistry class that he said he liked. His teachers wrote, "Chris has

said he is going to Job Corps, which may explain his lack of effort."
He wasn't going to class; when he did come, he wasn't prepared with
materials or assignments that he'd missed; and he had stopped seeking extra help after school.

Chris had skipped 67 classes by the time he got his Job Corps
assignment, on October 8. In many ways, he had long been ready to
go, but he was overwhelmed by his to-do list. He had to go shopping
to prepare for dorm life, he had to get clean in case he was asked to
take a drug test, and he had to drop out of school to properly enroll
in an academic program of the Job Corps, which he did on October
14. Mom considered the formalities of withdrawing from school a
bit too easy—nothing more than the stroke of a pen on a document
that acknowledged Chris' plans to continue his education elsewhere.
By the end of the short visit, the deal was done and he was moving
on with his life. No fuss, no frills.

The rest of the family joined them at the Joliet Job Corps Center
later that afternoon, and lined the back of a packed room where
an administrator was leading the new student orientation session.
"This place is no safe haven," she said. "The same mess that goes
on outside of this center occurs inside its walls—gangs, sex, fights,
pregnancy, theft, drugs." Chris seemed unmoved; he sat at a round
table with head bowed, busily marking the "intake" forms which he
had intercepted just as they brushed our mother's fingertips. After
reviewing the ins and outs of everyday life in the center, eight of us
trailed the group on a walking tour of the facilities, poking our heads
into classrooms of youthful Black and Brown bodies at work and
play. When Chris grabbed his suitcases—which were stuffed with the
necessities: new clothes and shoes, toiletries, iPod, journal, family
photos, cellphone, snacks—and continued on the last leg of the tour
in lively conversation with a boy he had met in school during his
freshman year, the rest of us moseyed back to our cars in quiet reflection. I felt a peculiar combination of grief, pride, and joy, as I might
have if we had sent him off to college or to war, but underneath these
feelings was the hard fact that we were there because he couldn't
have made it out of high school otherwise.

IN SEARCH OF CLUES

It had been 3 months since Chris left home and school for the Job Corps. All the while, the researcher in me was obsessively looking for clues about why, as if whatever I discovered might bring him back, redirect his course, give him a do-over. In bound journals, I kept notes—hundreds of pages of them—on my thinking and the thinking of others about my brother's educational biography. With my brother's consent, I secured copies of his personal documents—school progress reports, school punishment and attendance records, municipal citations and records of arrest, medical history, student services referral forms, and Job Corps application materials—from my mother, who, many years ago, began collecting copies for her own files. I pulled archival materials from the libraries in the two communities where he had grown up to juxtapose his story with a partial picture of the neighborhood and school backdrops that worked on and through him. I explored newspaper articles, yearbooks, district newsletters, district and school report cards, community historical guides and marketing materials, and U.S. Census reports, making handwritten comments to supplement my own recollection of what the communities were like at the time that we had lived there. I narrowed my focus to understanding what these documents could tell me about the villages' demography, municipal services and codes, recreation and social life, and the schools' policies and practices to get some sense of what was going on in the schools that my brother had attended. Finally, I asked a ton of questions of everybody in the family, and found out that it was my mother who had the juicy backstory.

The crucial part didn't come out right away. Mom first had to revisit the circumstances of my brother's birth, the wonder of his infancy, and the little guy he once was. She rehashed how we'd saved Chris from Royal and Roy Alexander (what my brother would have been named if I hadn't caused a ruckus); how Andrea and I used to soothe Chris in our arms by bouncing around our living room in tight circles for the full length of a Kris Kross album; how busy he once was with many pursuits—basketball, football, rollerskating, gymnastics, karate, freehand drawing, boxing, videogaming, and the trumpet; how he closed a school performance with a choreographed split, James Brown–style. Good times—the kind of family lore that I don't get tired of hearing.

I was listening closely though for the tipping point, which Mom said happened when Chris was in 4th grade. His teacher strongly suggested that Mom have him evaluated for Attention Deficit/ Hyperactivity Disorder (ADHD), a condition that Mom didn't know much about but that sounded too spooky to ignore. In February 2002, my mother found out that there are no physical markers or neurological tests to demonstrate the presence of ADHD. "It's more of an observation of the child," Mom recalled the family's pediatrician saying, and as far as the doctor could tell, "Christopher was just being an average boy, and the people in his life needed to get over it and get around it, including the teachers." Mom added, "He felt that the teachers nowadays were so quick to throw people"—mainly boys—"into the ADD pot."

How Chris Got Labeled

ADHD hit the books in the 1980s as a frequent diagnosis for people who have problems with inattention, hyperactivity, and impulsivity. In *Distinguishing Disability: Parents, Privilege, and Special Education*, Colin Ong-Dean (2009) documented the explosion in the number of children and adults diagnosed with ADHD. **There were about 900,000 people in the United States with the condition in 1991, when the U.S. Department of Education issued a memorandum that left it up to state and local education agencies to categorize their ADHD students as having a learning disability, emotional disturbance, or other health impairment; there were almost 5 million people with ADHD by 1997, when the condition was estimated by the American Academy of Child and Adolescent Psychiatry to be the most common category for referrals to child and adolescent psychiatric health services** (p. 82). Around the same time, the terms *ADHD* and its equivalent *ADD* entered the popular lexicon. A search of the online LexisNexis database, for example, cites nine articles in the *New York Times* that use the phrase *attention deficit disorder* between 1985 and 1989, 44 articles between 1990 and 1994, 147 articles between 1995 and 1999, 227 articles between 2000 and 2005, and 327 articles over the past 5 years. Absent social context, ADHD is a crossover hit about individuals' pathologies, and in the world of teaching and learning, there's a peculiar incentive to sing its tune.

Mom remembered telling our pediatrician, "Well, I don't know how boys are. I just know that this is what's going on: He is not being successful at school and the teachers are frustrated with him." And because at least some of the school's reports about Chris' inability to keep still or quiet seemed to jibe with what Mom had seen at home, the doctor offered a pharmacological treatment: Adderall, a stimulant composed of mixed amphetamine salts, to be taken most mornings, usually before school. For a number of reasons, Mom decided not to fill the prescription. In the first place, she came to share our physician's skepticism about the teachers' interpretations of Chris' behavior, and she considered the stake that the school officials had in Chris returning to class under medical treatment suspect. Sometimes, she believed that the disorder itself was bogus, a foolproof way to identify "bad kids" and account for their undereducation. And when she found out that drugs such as Adderall can cause nervousness, headaches, sleeplessness, and decreased appetite, among other side effects, and that amphetamines have a high potential for abuse and can lead to dependence, she figured that medicating Chris wasn't worth the risk. Instead, she began working more closely with him on schoolwork and increasing her own visibility in the school building: two reliable strategies that were informed by her own background in education. She had once been a student—a remarkable one—at a selective enrollment high school and later at Northwestern University, where she trained to be an elementary school teacher. Despite all of Mom's efforts, Chris' principal, a stern nun from the East Coast, cited his misbehavior and immaturity—not his grades—as justification for retention. He was ultimately promoted to the 5th grade without delay, but it took some finagling. "I told her not only would I go to the archdiocese about her, but I would go to Operation PUSH because I felt it was a racial issue," Mom said. My mother was on to something.

When Chris was 10, he enrolled at a parochial school, where he got a teacher who "was crazy," in Mom's estimation. Mom likened her to Sally Field's character in the 1976 film *Sybil*, which was based on the true story of a young woman whose own mother cloaked emotional and physical abuse in religious practices that brought on Sybil's multiple personality disorder. Mom said, "One of the things she used to do is make her drink a whole lot of water, chain her to the piano and sit there and play the piano and force the girl to hold this water," that she would eventually be punished for releasing. When Mom walked into my brother's classroom one morning and the teacher was alone playing the piano, the resemblance was eerie.

Mom remembered listening to the teacher yell at the kids in the classroom—Chris on one particular occasion—while she waited unannounced outside the door. When Mom made her presence known, the teacher's biting "I don't have your paper. You're lying!" turned into an angelic "I don't know what would've happened to your paper." Mom complained to the school principal and board president about the teacher and suggested that the building's intercom system be used to monitor her classes, but again, Mom thought it was better for Chris to finish the year there and keep moving.

Mom and I had been sitting together for over an hour, and her descriptions of Chris' early schooling experiences became simpler, the details thinner. "So in 6th grade, he went to another Catholic school that didn't have a nun for a principal," she said. The school was run by a lay staff under the direction of an African American woman who hailed from Chicago. "I ended up taking him out of there midyear because she wanted me to take him out and stuff because he was causing too much problems in the class." Mom had little else to say about how Chris had spent his time at the school or the circumstances of his departure, but she made it clear that his leaving had not been on bad terms. "She actually told me some things and I ended up getting some good information from her." The principal told Mom that there is a federal law protecting the specific educational rights of children with disabilities and, considering Chris' ADHD diagnosis, he might qualify for some support in public schools that private schools do not have to provide; she then directed Mom to the district office of her neighborhood school.

Mom got a whole new understanding of ADHD when she met with a school psychologist. Whereas ADHD is typically thought to be a problem of inattention, he explained to her that people with ADHD actually pay attention to everything; they do not have tunnel vision. The way in which he described the disorder seemed to resonate with what Mom had observed in Chris. "It was weird because I started seeing Christopher in a new light. The stuff that [the doctor] was saying was kind of right on." Like the school principal who'd referred Mom to him, the school psychologist let her in on a quietly kept secret. He helped her make sense of ADHD, Mom said, "what it was and what it meant, and what I could demand the schools do for Chris." Pushing the schools to acknowledge and accommodate his differences was an uphill battle that Mom would struggle with in the years to come, but at that time, she was conflicted about the possibility that Chris may have legitimately been sick, and without the medication that he needed to get well. "I wasn't really sold on medicine—definitely not ADHD medicine—but, I definitely didn't want my son not to be successful," she said.

Going through Chris' files, we found a copy of an email that Mom had sent to our pediatrician, dated February 9, 2004, in which she requested the medication that he had offered 2 years before:

Christopher has been having trouble in school. He is failing all his major subjects. These are the type of things that his teachers have reported:

Does not complete his work
Extremely short attention span
Having trouble retaining information
Behavior problems
Unable to keep still or keep quiet
Unable to concentrate or stay on task
Making noises and disturbing the class

If asked why he did something, Christopher responds that he doesn't know why.

Christopher will be attending his fourth school in 3 years. He was expelled from [school] last week because the principal felt that the teachers there were unable to teach Christopher. He is a very nice and mannerable boy. He is not violent, nor does he have problems fighting with others. He appears to be obsessed with the social aspect of school and not the work. He loves to draw and is very intricate with his drawings. He can sit for hours and play videogames but can only do school work for 2 minutes. He constantly frustrates his teachers. Every teacher that Christopher has had in the last 3 years says he can do the work. They do not feel that he needs additional tutoring. I have worked with Christopher and I know how hard it is to keep him on task. I spoke briefly with a school psychologist, and he says it sounds more like ADHD than a learning disability. I am scheduling Christopher to be tested for learning disabilities. While I wait for this to be done, I would like to start him on the ADHD medication. I am open to all suggestions.

Barbara

Chris' 6th-grade report card looks a lot like mine from the neighborhood school that my sister and I attended. His homeroom teacher was Miss Z. and she'd marked him absent three times. His reading teacher made detailed comments, but I can't make out the handwriting, which is unfortunate because the information might have helped me understand why Chris was recorded as having finished the year reading at a 5th-grade level yet met current standards in language arts. In fact, he did okay in each of his classes; he earned mostly B's and C's and a couple of A's, and he got high scores in the other performance areas listed. The noted exceptions were that he appeared to go about formulating and solving math problems in his own way rather than using agreed-upon operations and strategies, that he daydreamed, and that he had no sense of time—finishing work on time, coming to school on time, and using class time constructively. At the bottom there is a section, "Message to Parents," in which Miss Z.

wrote, "Chris is a joy to have in class. He is very respectful. Good job!!" under Third Quarter, and beneath Fourth Quarter, "Have a great summer!!" In recognition of his efforts, Miss Z. attached a bare outline of a puppy on half a page of baby-blue paper that has the words *DOGGONE GOOD!* printed on it.

Something happened to Chris the following year, although it's not clear what. "There wasn't a lot of positives after 6th grade," Mom told me. "He wasn't really doing a whole lot. Most of the teachers would always say the same thing, 'Oh, he *can* do it. He just *won't* do it.'" Sometimes medication—and even the Adderall that Mom once disguised as multivitamins—seemed to help muster his willpower. She told me, "I wasn't happy with the extra side effects that went along with it, you know, because he really did not sleep well and he definitely was not eating well because that was—it's speed. It takes away your appetite and it makes you jumpy and jittery." He was a handsome little guy of 12—less than 5 feet tall and 95 pounds—but pictures from this time reflect a striking seriousness in his expression.

I was studying in New York City when Chris moved with the family to a house that backs against a creek on a road of imposing homes, but I'd heard about him through the grapevine. Family gossip said that Chris was flouting cardinal rules at home, hanging out late with the boys in the old neighborhood, and spending more time studying cultural representations of hip-hop—music, clothes, hairstyles, body art, lingo, dances, and poses—than his schoolbooks; his grades reveal that this scenario had more than a glimmer of truth. Having missed only 3 days of school during the first semester of 8th grade, he had managed six F's, four D's, three C's, and one B. "I said: No, I'm not going out of my way to be driving you over there and you not handling the business," Mom told me. "So that's how he ended up at [the neighborhood junior high school]"—a four-block walk from the house. He narrowly finished the school year.

In a 2006 family photograph that includes Chris, Mom, and Roy, I see a familiar image of proud parents posing at an elementary school graduation. Roy, dressed in a brown patterned shirt and dark slacks, hovers over the right side of Chris, who is standing with his head tilted atop a stiffened neck, pressing the cover of his diploma against his opposite hip underneath arms that are hanging toward the floor. Chris wears a dark pinstriped shirt so long that his trousers are beyond the frame of the shot. An American flag rests on the raised stage behind him. Mom leans into his left shoulder. Both her bright gold blouse and the blue and white ribbons in her hand have a bit of sheen. The position of the ribbons (which Chris had added as adornment to his gown), clutched as high as her chest somewhere between her and Chris, suggests a desire to hold on to the fleeting moment when, half an hour before, his name had been read from a list of graduates. Chris and Mom gaze directly toward their audience with wide smiles, while Roy stares out, as if he is being photographed by another camera.

As I look closer at the picture, I can see that my mother's big brown eyes are worn and narrow, rimmed with dark circles that mimic her freckled cheeks. Near the end of our talk, she told me, "Christopher has a lot of knowledge that he don't even realize is in that noggin," and considering his early schooling, "I don't know how it got in there." But on second thought, the lessons Mom had taught Chris about confronting and negotiating institutions that denigrate and invalidate his sense of worth—or what feminist scholar Patricia Hill Collins (1994) might more aptly consider her "motherwork"—had to count for something: **"I just didn't want him to be defeated and thinking that he couldn't do nothing or that he was dumb, which is what happens to a lot of young Black kids and I just was fighting like hell to make sure that he wasn't one of those." I can see the exhaustion of this struggle—to affirm her son's survival, power, and identity in educational spaces—in her eyes.**

★   ★   ★

Freshman year is a pivotal, make-or-break time for students, when few who veer off track get back on path to graduate. At the start of the second semester of Chris' 9th-grade year, my mother reached out to his school for guidance. He'd failed each of the three courses for which he was registered the previous term, he'd seen the Dean seven times, and he'd met with a school counselor on one occasion. By his own admission, Chris had not completed most of his schoolwork, and according to his teachers, he'd made a practice of disrupting class—talking excessively, walking around, swearing, refusing to sign detention forms, and otherwise deflecting responsibility for his actions. Something had to give, and because my mother was somewhat suspicious that Chris had long suffered from ADHD, she looked to the school to evaluate her son's academic progress. She requested that his teachers and Pupil Personnel Services—a team comprised of an administrator, psychologist, counselor, and dean—dig up his files and keep an eye on him in the weeks that followed.

Twelve days into the New Year, Chris seemed to be doing all right, aside from a few missing assignments, but when Mom met with Pupil Personnel Services on January 18, 2007, the detailed report of a former teacher gave the conference a stale air. The teacher wrote that Chris "Taps, gets up & talks nonstop" and that he's "easily distracted"—patterned discoveries that Mom expected to discuss, but there was more. She described his class participation as "Passive, [because he] never brings material," "Average," "Enthusiastic," and "Dominant, if [he is] in his hyper mode," and nonexistent, "if [he's] angry." She wrote that Chris shows no initiative—he neither works well independently nor seeks additional help—yet he "strives to divert others from learning" and "Often they do enjoy the chaos he causes, but sometimes they do not." She added that he is immature, belligerent, and disruptive. "Anger or astonishment follows any corrections by the teacher." And finally, when asked for recommendations on ways to address Chris' difficulties and enhance his performance, the teacher wrote: "He must begin to care about his education, get a handle on what successful students do, and he must find a way to stay focused or he will continue to squander opportunities for advancement." Insofar as Pupil Personnel Services was concerned, Chris wasn't disabled; he was a troublemaker, and there wasn't a thing that the school could do about that. Mom took their notes and began making some of her own.

Over the next 5 months, she researched the nuances of special education decisionmaking and law to learn how to make the school acknowledge and provide some support for Chris' needs. She read legal statutes that include disabled children in public education and outline some standards for the quality of their education: Section 504 of the Rehabilitation Act of 1973 and parts of the Education for All Handicapped Children Act of 1975 (EAHCA) and its successor, the Individuals with Disabilities Education Act of 2004 (IDEA). Mom asked around and looked online, and when she found that ADHD is recognized as a condition that might have qualified Chris for educational accommodations (such as modified teacher practices associated with academic instruction, behavioral interventions, and the physical classroom environment), her desire to give him whatever advantages a disability label may have provided began to outweigh its implications. Meanwhile, Chris' own studies produced another set of quarterly results—two F's and a C, in music—that strengthened her resolve.

It had been more than a year since Chris had taken Adderall when Mom received the final grade report for his freshman year. Within weeks, she toted him to the new pediatrician, who had taken over our family doctor's practice after his retirement, for another prescription. Mom explained to the new doctor much of what I've relayed above. He took copious notes, but with no record of a recent prescription in Chris' chart, and given his newness on the job, it behooved him to begin the diagnostic process again. Mom and Chris left that June 2007 visit with paperwork and a sense of how things would unfold. Chris would be observed in multiple settings—by my mother at home and by two of his classroom teachers at school. The assessment used would be the National Initiative for Child Healthcare Quality (NICHQ) Vanderbilt forms—simple scoring sheets that would tell the pediatrician about the ways in which Chris experienced core symptoms of ADHD, the age of onset and duration of symptoms, the level of functional impairment, and whether there were other coexisting conditions. Once the forms were completed, an ADHD subtype would be determined—either predominantly inattentive, predominantly hyperactive, or both—and a management plan would be crafted around my brother's particular needs.

In his medical files, I see that during an August follow-up Chris complained of persistent tailbone pain and zits, and he talked about his diet of Pop-Tarts, nachos, fries, and pizza, but there is little mention of the evaluation. By mid-September, someone from the Special Programs Department at Chris' high school had faxed copies of all three informants' forms to the pediatrician's office. The conversation opened with a discussion of a stressor in Chris' life—our maternal grandparents' cancers—and to the side effects of Adderall. It closed with Chris obtaining a prescription for Strattera, an antidepressant that was thought to be a more gradual and long-term approach to managing his disorder, and directions to check in with the doctor once a week to assess his tolerance of the medication.

Strattera is known to cause nausea, dizziness, lassitude, and allergic reactions, among other things, especially during the first few weeks of treatment. An FDA warning on Strattera's label notes that it can lead to heart problems, liver damage, and suicidal thinking. In early October, Chris was eating and sleeping well, and he had enough energy after school to train with a local boxing club every now and then. He had some trouble remembering to swallow each capsule whole with a meal at the same time every day, but with Mom's help that seemed to be working out fine, too. Physically, Chris was feeling like himself; psychosomatically, he was having a hard time.

In 2002, when educators claimed that Chris had difficulty learning, my mother had been skeptical; 5 years later, when a paper trail enabled his disability to be identified, it was my brother who seriously doubted its legitimacy. Chris told me once, "Don't nobody just want to sit there and look at the same stuff," and if we understand ADHD in this way—as a problem of inattentiveness to "the same stuff"—then the disorder must be even more widespread than we think. "Everybody has it." Even if we see the disorder from another of my brother's lenses—as a tendency to pay attention to everything—then Chris figured that he isn't disabled; he is gifted. "Everybody ain't like that." Whatever it means, Chris gave up any pretense that he could be convinced by good arguments on either side. "I'm a regular kid," he told me, which is why he couldn't make sense of all of the fuss around him at school.

Pupil Personnel Services documented the pediatrician's diagnosis: Chris had ADHD, a condition that is classified as a disability by the state of Illinois under the category of "other health impairment." However, the team found that his symptoms were not severe enough to call for specialized instruction, the procedural requirements for which are controlled by the Individuals with Disabilities Education Act. His disorder seemed manageable with reasonable accommodations, such as coteaching as a means for providing him with special educational services in general education classrooms. Mom had no objections to this arrangement. She said, "They explained to me that cotaught classes would be that while the one teacher is teaching [content], the other is really focusing on the [the learning processes of] students." Students would be heterogeneously grouped in various sizes and both equally licensed teachers would work with each student. No one would know about Chris' disability or the fact that he was receiving special services.

The assumption of discretion was paramount to Chris. He had made a name for himself as someone who was sharp and capable, but fearlessly engaged in a struggle of wills with authority; somewhere within the labyrinth of a social scene at the high school, that was cool. It was in this small space of belonging, of authenticity, and of power that he believed he'd kept his head above water. Being exposed as disabled, with all of the explanations and expectations that a difference signifies, would have done more than cramp his style; it would have destroyed his integrity.

★   ★   ★

A disability speaks. It says something not just about a person's impairment, but also about the person himself. It tells us that he is somehow different from other people; he is abnormal. The imprint of a disability and the meanings that it carries is more than enough for a person to bear, but there is more for someone whose difference is shunned: He is stigmatized. He has to confront and be affronted with people who think about, look at, talk to, and treat him differently, and who use the disability as a lens to do so. He may be acutely aware of how he sees himself and how others see him; he senses that others don't really receive him on equal grounds, and sometimes he tells himself that this is justifiable. A disabled person is not just marked; he is disqualified from full social acceptance, what sociologist Erving Goffman (1963) described in his book *Stigma: Notes on the Management of Spoiled Identity* as being "discredited." The situation is precarious for a disabled person, which is why many people with disabilities do not identify themselves as such (Watson, 2002).

Goffman (1963) tells us that a person with a disability is exceptionally self-conscious and calculating about the impression he makes. He may feel that he is "on," hypersensitive to his own thinking and the thinking of others, and unable to be himself in social surrounds. **He notices when others undermine the ordinary scheme of things by exaggerating his small accomplishments or when minor failings are attributed to his difference, and when either interaction brings him undue attention, he feels violated. His character is shamed, his privacy invaded.**

A disabled person seeks communion. He might reach out to "the wise" people in his life who are not disabled but whose relationship to him have made them intimately privy to his circumstances. He leans on his "own" kind and comes together in small groups for love and affirmation with sympathetic others who share the stigma. In these refuges of self-defense, he may "openly take the line that he is at least as good as anyone else" (Goffman, 1963, p. 145). Ultimately, he strives to jettison his difference by attempting to correct the disability, but if such a repair is impossible, he may try to master an area of activity that is an unlikely association with the disability or he may reinterpret the nature of the disability. Keeping a low profile is central to covering signs of disability, but he may also fight mightily the stigma and what it reveals about him.

I'm reminded of my brother and his oscillation from recognition to rejection of his disability, and anyone who bought into it. "Sometimes I feel like I do [have ADHD], but okay, just because I have ADD, that don't have nothing to do with anything," Chris told me. "Mama always use that ADD stuff as an excuse to get me out of stuff. I hate that!" For him, it was a crutch and a myth that helped other people manage tensions around his problems. Chris thought the disability had chosen him. "He just cannot get over the stigma that his generation has attached to ADD and he feels really appalled to be in that classification," Mom told me. ADHD was embarrassing and insulting, and "the thought of special ed just made him want to lay on the floor and just give up," Mom said. Layer this with the crisis of adolescence and the particular implications of Black masculinity, and his experience must have been especially complicated.

★   ★   ★

I am trying to remember more. In November 2007, Mom and Chris met with his English teacher to discuss his mid-semester progress. As chance would have it, the English teacher belonged to the same department as the teacher who'd provided Pupil Personnel Services with an unflattering account of Chris' academic performance the previous school year. Chris was anxious about the meeting partly because he knew that he hadn't picked up much in her class. "I know how to write a sentence. I know how to write paragraphs and shit like that, but when it comes to big stuff like I can't even remember English," he admitted. "Like what you do in English?" he asked me. What the English teacher told Mom Chris did was: "Refuse to follow through on instructions and finish assignments, avoid tasks that require sustained mental effort, and talk excessively." Chris lingered just beyond the classroom's doorway, which muffled much of what the teacher reported. However, when she said to Mom, "I got 20-something kids and I don't have time to deal with so many that have issues, who need to be in special ed," Chris said he heard as clear as day, "He don't need to be in here. He's retarded." Having spent years taking baby steps toward the margins of school life, this incident pushed him take a giant leap off its precipice. Chris told me, "That made me want to drop out."

My mother's visceral reaction to "pummel that woman" was tempered by a more reasoned response. Mom told me that when she had trained to be a teacher in the 1970s, she'd learned that "Educators are taught to teach to the mainstream," and that those students who fall below or above the curve make educators earn their keep. To be sure, many teachers are underpaid, overworked, and unprepared to meet some of the challenges of everyday life in schools; this is, at least in part, what led Mom to choose a different line of work. "They allow and expect some castoff," Mom told me. "They are okay if five or six of them are just sitting there sucking up air." Her son would not be one of them. The following day, Mom kept Chris home from school, and she called the district as well as the Illinois State Board of Education to find out the legalities of finishing his high school education under her charge. She could hardly believe that she didn't have to do much more than say—well, write a letter saying—that she would be home schooling him, but she withdrew Chris from high school anyway in an attempt to teach him on her own. Mom looked to friends and family members, including me, for help, and she searched the Internet for information about state guidelines, curriculum planning, and teaching in general. But she had enough on her plate: She was already strained by the responsibilities at her full-time job, her side hustle as a real estate agent and developer, and caring for two aging parents in addition to the calls of duty at home that included being a wife, a mother, and a provider for my siblings, as well as a grandmother and babysitter for my sister's two young children. Being the sole educator and primary social contact for Chris every day was not happening; things never quite got off the ground. He stayed home for one quarter, then returned and failed each of his classes. And then Mom's parents died.

*   *   *

In 2008, the high school district began to restructure each of its three underperforming schools, including my brother's. Scores in reading and math did not pass the muster on state achievement tests; poor and Black students did especially badly; and the school had not once made Adequate Yearly Progress toward the goal of all students reaching academic standards since the No Child Left Behind Act of 2001 had been enacted. The district was on the upswing of a financial crisis that had set in 10 years earlier, when decreasing revenues, failed tax increase referendums, and a stalling local economy had threatened the district's tax base. It sorely needed to make some changes, especially in school governance. The superintendent saw restructuring as an opportunity to create strong schools that could prepare young people to compete in a global market. The Illinois State Board of Education had been watching the district's schools, along with one-third of all other public schools in the Prairie State that had fallen short on testing standards that year, and via teleconference it relayed a frank and chilling message: "[The] district has been failing students for the last 5 years." The state added an incentive for the district to shake things up: Either improve test scores or lose oversight of the schools.

In January 2008, when the district announced its intention to draw up improvement plans, it reduced the school day, cut athletic and extracurricular programs, and blocked the bell schedule. When school started again in September of that year, the district had restored the length of the school day, adopted a new reading course and math program, refurbished resource rooms for special education students, and returned to a seven-period schedule.

Chris spent much of the first day of his third year at the school with Mom in the office of the Special Programs Department chair, selecting his classes. They arranged a schedule of five classes: Four of the five classes were cotaught; one of the four provided supplementary services to students with disabilities. Chris recounted the story as we talked over the phone. "The line was long and they was turning people away—telling people that they had to make an appointment—but you know Mama!" Chris said. Mom bypassed the counselors who were stationed at tables handing out computer-generated schedules, and she went directly to the Special Programs Department, with Chris in tow, to revise his schedule.

His schedule would include a combination of classes that he'd failed in previous years and some at grade level. He'd work on reading and writing skills in English, social studies in U.S. History, science in Chemistry, and mathematics in Algebra. She tried to squeeze in a vocational elective like Auto Shop or Radio and Television, but either it was not available or did not fit the schedule. He took PE. The program of study was meticulously designed to prepare Chris for a series of GED tests, although where he would sit for them was somewhat of a mystery. He had plans to join the fall 2008 class of cadets at the Lincoln's Challenge Academy, where, according to the Special Programs Department chair, many students from the high school had already gone. But then Chris heard enough about the intensity of the military model undergirding Lincoln's Challenge Academy to know that it was not the best fit for him, and soon word came about the Job Corps. Chris chomped at the bit. The high school didn't put up a fight. And the rest, as cliché goes, is history.

CHAPTER 4

21 Questions

MY BROTHER'S 21ST BIRTHDAY fell on a Thursday, close enough to Friday for him to justifiably stretch the celebration across the span of an entire weekend. Being a woman in my 30s and having officially aged out of the youth movement, I was kindly excluded from most of the festivities. I did hear that at the stroke of midnight, Chris shoved some pocket change into a slot machine at a nearby casino—not because he's much of a gambler, but for the plain fact that legally he could—and afterward a private party in the casino's hotel kept him up for hours. When I saw him later, he glowed. Chris was freshly showered and shaved, dressed to the nines, smiling from ear to ear, giddy to jumpstart his first night out on the town as a bona fide adult.

But before he could dance, he had to sing. He had to hover over a candlelit cake, surrounded by ogling family and friends, both embarrassed and amused, belting out a silly declaration of just how old he was. "I'm 21 years old. I'm 21 years old. I'm 21 years old. I'm 21 years old." It's a tradition, and yes, in our family, birthdays are kind of a big deal. No matter how old (or theologically doubtful) we may get, the good Lord is always asked—in unison, emphatically, with fake sneezes and all—to bless the birthday boy or girl. Then a hush falls over the crowd. It is time to make a wish, to silently dream of anything, even the virtually impossible. Chris lowered his head, closed his eyes, and said, "You already know." I didn't, of course, but I think I do now.

From the looks of things, I'd venture to say he plunged into prayer, hoping that there was a generous and forgetful god somewhere losing count of the fourth and fifth chances she has indiscriminately given him. Chris swayed, mouthing words that nobody in the room could overhear as we waited, curiously and patiently, for him to finish. It was a completely different spectacle from the one I had observed around this time a little more than 5 years ago. In a room at the back of a small church near our home, the entire family settled into a row of metal chairs a quarter of the way back from the edge of a raised platform where Chris sat fixed on the service ahead. He was slightly slouched with head cocked to the right and hands in his lap; he spoke few words to the nine other baptism candidates who lined his left side.

"Take me to the water," the members began to croon in a low hum.

Chris did not know much about the practice of religion or about what life would be like after the baptism. He'd agreed to go through with it anyway because "it made Mama happy," he told me, and if our mother had been privy to his indifference, she seemed unconcerned about it. Mom had begun to lean more heavily on her faith after her parents passed away, and although her religiosity didn't seem to take to the rest of us similarly, her gift of gab never fails to pacify our apprehensions and hesitation. By the time the rest of the family heard about the idea, Chris had been listed on the program and was preparing for the ceremony.

"Take me to the water," the members repeated.

An elderly Black woman extended both arms in his direction. As Chris filed slowly toward the steps that flanked the lap pool where, in tall rubber boots, the pastor awaited, I watched him attentively in wonder and disbelief. What was he thinking? Was this real? Was something stirring inside him? His face revealed nothing, except maybe lethargy. Chris disappeared behind thick curtains.

"Take me to the water to be baptized," the members chanted.

Chris reemerged, peaceful and subdued, wrapped in pure white garb. Like the others who had gone before him, he eased into the symbolic waters of the Jordan and, without pause, made a public commitment to live the rest of his days in the image of God.

"What's your name?"

"Christopher."

"What has Jesus done for you?"

"Died for my sins."

"What are you going to do for Jesus?"

"Praise him every day."

Mom did intend to get Chris closer to God, although her plan was also something of a ruse. Chris was 15 years old, equal parts bravado and humility, and considered by loved ones to be smart, bright, and plummeting down a rabbit hole. She had sought the direction of teachers and school counselors, medical doctors, lawyers, a budding educational researcher, and now God. She'd staged an intervention that openly recognized a need for help, and Chris played along. "I just feel like I got dunked in some water. I ain't feel nothing really, not like I was a new person," he told me. In fact, he admitted, "I don't really believe in gods."

That was then—before he dropped out of school, before graduating from the Job Corps to part-time work selling shoes, before he found himself and the Holy Spirit in Cook County Jail.

★   ★   ★

Besides this book, the hardest thing I have ever written was the letter I sent to Chris on his 20th birthday. There were no suitable words for such an occasion. My kitchen table was littered with crumpled notebook paper on which I had scrawled faint humor, poetic fluffiness, and unhelpful conjecture about light-filled tunnels when I decided to say what I felt, which was something on the order of "This sucks; we miss you a lot." It wasn't deep, but I thought that Chris would appreciate the simplicity, and since little else competed for his attention, I presumed that he would read the note often.

Chris plowed through all the reading materials he could get his hands on. Hip-hop magazines and urban fiction novels were his favorites. When he wasn't reading or sleeping or otherwise loafing around, he was whipping up and bartering the culinary creations he made from the junk food available in the commissary. County Cakes took a mound of anything sweet. Pizza Puffs called for soggy bread slices, scrap meat, and ketchup packages. Hot Noodle Soup was cold but spiced with a bag of Cheetos crumbs. Penal conditions induce resourcefulness, but what an active imagination it must have required of him to come up with and eat some of this stuff.

I, the schoolmarm, wanted Chris to take a class. What kind did not matter all that much to me, but Chris wouldn't have it. As I pressed the issue during a visit, he explained his resistance to the idea quite adamantly. First, he said, his "Good Enough Degree"—his GED—was more than good enough for what he was doing at that moment. Touché. Though, for what it is worth, I have seen some evidence that educational programs run in correctional settings can be beneficial to those who participate in them. There is nothing conclusive, but research suggests that correctional education can reduce recidivism—meaning, the chances of re-offense, rearrest, and re-incarceration—and can increase employment potential after release. Now, that's no conciliation for Chris. An abstract possibility for an uncertain future wouldn't radically change the circumstances of being locked up, but I thought it was important to at least consider how correctional school might qualitatively shape his experience.

CORRECTIONAL EDUCATION

Somewhere I read that correctional schooling can make incarcerated students more motivated, more confident, happier people. Given the day-to-day living conditions in jails and prisons, Chris certainly could have used a boost. While Chris was in the County, my two greatest concerns were always for his safety and his sanity. Exaggerated scenes on network TV, combined with my own refusal to ask Chris what things were really like, made me see the threat of violence and going crazy as incessant. It does happen. Overcrowding and extreme isolation coexist. Gangs are active. Racial segregation, hostility, and racism are allowed and, in many places, institutionally sanctioned.

What is truer is that incarcerated people are often so bored out of their minds that they busy themselves with mischief or lose touch with reality and the outside world. Taking a class would give Chris something productive to hang onto, and I expected him to want to sign up. But, for more reasons than one, he didn't.

Second, Chris said, a college transcript listing Cook County Jail as his school of higher learning would do him no favors. I may have wholeheartedly agreed with Chris on this point if only that were the case, which it isn't. Typical of detention centers across the country, Cook County Jail does not even offer postsecondary education. Some form of GED or high school preparation, vocational training, and life skills programming are usually available, but not college courses. If the county did have a degree-granting program, then an accredited community college or university would administer it, and also sign, seal, and deliver any paperwork earned. But sadly, if the waitlist to enroll in such a course of study happened to be shorter than my brother's projected stay, the violent crimes that Chris has been charged with committing would likely disqualify him from getting one of the coveted spots anyway. Here is yet another frustrating daily routine for incarcerated people: picking up, taking in, and recycling pieces of misinformation.

Why Chris did not know or understand the resources and services that were available to him while in custody is as big a problem as his reluctance to take advantage of them. My own speculation falls on operational malfunction, a breakdown in the system. Cook County Jail is gigantic, with ten divisions that span more than eight city blocks, employing a staff of 3,800 and holding an average daily population of 9,000. An enterprise of this size and complexity is bound to have some administrative missteps, and some haters, too. Criminals won't do better if they know better—that's the pessimistic nonsense that many people who live or work inside jails and prisons actually believe. Other incarcerated individuals often look unfavorably toward and put peer pressure on individuals whom they perceive as trying to advance themselves. Officers—many of them having little more than a high school diploma—see inmates, especially those in college programs, as unfair competition and undeserving beneficiaries. According to one group of researchers, "Many jail and prison staff members will tell you quite forthrightly that they do not think that prisoners should be allowed to pursue 'free education'" (Werner, Widestrom, & Pues, 2012, p. 74). The received wisdom about imprisonment as punishment, along with the implications it carries for getting along in the real world, reflects a broader consensus. Ask anyone about the purpose of incarceration and I would bet that "education" is unlikely to be cited; the common response "to teach a lesson" does not count.

Besides experiencing a reality check and poor communication, my brother gave a third reason for passing on the idea of taking a course that abruptly ended our discussion: Chris said with all seriousness that he was too dumb to function in a classroom, even one full of jailbirds. The statement wasn't a crash in confidence or an invitation to a pity party; I took it as an honest self-assessment of what he thought he was and was not capable of. Unsure of what I was supposed to do with his confession, I bowed out and changed the subject.

Incidentally, I later got an email from a friend and colleague about a workshop she wanted us to cofacilitate for members of the Correctional Education Association. The group was to meet in central Illinois for 2 days of professional development on a wide array of topics that the correctional teachers who were expected to show up might find helpful. Several sections of workshops had been planned to cover recent changes in the field of correctional education, program offerings at adult and juvenile facilities in the Midwest and successful practices in classroom instruction. The conference program was ready for print when organizers noticed a gaping hole in the agenda: No one would be there to talk about the issue of poverty and how correctional teachers might better meet the needs of their students from low-income backgrounds. A Google search cited some pieces that my friend had published debunking the "culture of poverty" theory (which attributes poor people's conditions to their own ways of being) and they reached out to her pronto. She, in turn, contacted me: one, for company during the lackluster drive from the big city to the sticks, and two, to bring my perspective on the school-to-prison pipeline to bear on the exchange. Mind you, neither of us had ever heard of the Correctional Education Association, and with all due respect to our comrades who dare to teach behind the walls, our daily grind to transform public schools is intended to put them out of work. We saw a rare opportunity in attending their training, though, to spark some intradisciplinary dialogue and, for me, to get the inside scoop on what my brother was dodging.

The first thing that I noticed about the conference was how few people looked like us. Of the 200–250 people at the opening keynote, there may have been a handful of color. I assumed this to be typical of the teaching force in corrections, but during the formalities of that session—the welcome, acknowledgments, thanks, and housekeeping details—I was on my smartphone looking for stats. I didn't come across anything recent—still haven't—that breaks down the demographics of teachers on the payroll of correctional institutions, but I did learn that officers are the largest group of correctional workers, and that historically, correctional officers have been White males from rural areas and small towns.

The keynote speaker, Lois Davis of the RAND Corporation, a public policy think tank, got my attention with her slideshow presentation of the preliminary findings from a research project she was leading. The RAND Corporation and its partner, the Correctional Education Association, had been awarded a sizable grant from the U.S. Department of Justice to study the current state of correctional education and where it is heading. I was aware of the fact that not every person in jail and prison has access to education and that not every person with access has *high-quality* programming available. But it hadn't occurred to me for one second that the educational programs up and running in nearly all federal and state prisons and a significant number of local jails (however skimpy they may be) had been developed and administered based on sketchy or no empirical evidence. Such is the case, Davis explained. It turns out that we know very little about what the programs look like in terms of curricula and methods, staffing and quality of instruction, participation and completion rates, and other components that vary widely across facilities. Much of what is known comes from two national surveys, administered by the Bureau of Justice Statistics on a roughly 5-year cycle, that ask few questions about educational programs—which means that data are often outdated or missing. This also means that folks in the field of criminal justice—not education—have contributed the lion's share of information. Recently, several qualitative studies conducted by educationalists have begun to richly describe the nuances of teaching and learning inside correctional facilities (Fine et al., 2001; Winn, 2011; Winterfield, Coggeshall, Burker-Storer, Correa, & Tidd, 2009), but examples of this scholarship are few and far between.

I have thought long and hard about how this can be, and about what the lack of educationalists' perspectives means for the intellectual conversation around correctional education. Of course, the dearth of information about the scale, effectiveness, and implications of education programs offered in prisons and jails may account for education researchers' relative silence on the topic. But I also see the failure to study correctional education as a kind of willful public ignorance (Meiners, 2007; Mills, 1997), nudged by at least three groups of stakeholders in the education community—the public, mainstream educational institutions, and education researchers themselves. Stay with me here: Disinvestment in federal funding for correctional education programming, buttressed by waning public interest in rehabilitative approaches to corrections, means that there is hardly any centralized correctional education for education researchers to study. Moreover, many traditional education institutions and the people in them—K–12 schoolteachers, administrators, teacher educators, and others within university settings—tend to dismiss correctional education scholarship as beyond the scope of their immediate utility. After all, these folks are interested in moving youth along pipelines of success, not in lending credence to folklore and writings that document schools' complicity in pipelines to prison. It is likely also true that scholars and activists who are working to dismantle relationships between systems of education and criminal justice find an inherent tension in legitimizing-by-studying the correctional education enterprise, and that other education researchers generally avoid the study of teaching and learning in correctional settings because it has not yet been situated as a recognized subfield within the education profession. In short, the groups of stakeholders to which education researchers are most accountable offer limited incentives for scholars to confound their studies with correctional education.

Nonetheless, in 2011, Lois Davis and her team began a much-needed, federally funded, multiphase evaluation of correctional programs by interviewing groups of leaders in the field at a Correctional Education Association conference. Davis was at this conference to give an update on the results. Across the focus groups, participants had an awful lot to say about key challenges facing correctional education; their concerns about the effects of the economic downturn and budget cuts have stuck with me. Financial backing for correctional education comes from several sources, including state legislature monies, state departments of labor and education, federal grants, private or nonprofit organizations, and "inmate welfare" funds—code for profits turned from prison labor. Regardless of how money does get funneled downstream to pay for programs, the research participants worried that, at this time of shrinking resources, there is not very much of it to go around.

They complained about not having enough funding to hire staff, even when teachers retire or otherwise leave positions vacant, and that existing staff are stretched too thinly with heavy teaching loads, plus record-keeping and reporting on a flighty student body. One administrator said, "I'm down to 11 academic teachers in eight different buildings; how much more can you cut?" They were transparent about the implications of budget pressures, not just on teachers and their work experiences, but also on program operation and success. Representatives from some states admitted to making tough trade-offs and exploring imperfect alternatives, such as using students as peer tutors; eliminating efforts to purchase technology and upgrade computers; maintaining the number of program slots but reducing the amount of instructional time and program length; decreasing the number of students who receive programming, which, parenthetically, is already lousy; providing programming only to those individuals for whom it is court-ordered; and contracting correctional education out to private companies altogether. That last option—inviting a greater presence of private corporations into public facilities—is a controversial move, seen by some taxpayers as a rip-off and others as a boon. Davis' research participants didn't leverage arguments on either side, but they did express concerns about privatized programs, particularly when it came to recruiting, hiring, and retaining good people to work in them. Evidently, contract instructors are less likely to be certified, often earn less than teachers who are public employees, and, as one respondent put it, tend to "leave as soon as they get a job with benefits."

My friend and I started passing notes like schoolgirls, surprised that the conference had already raised so many issues of eerie familiarity. The racial and cultural divide between teachers and students, the problems of funding, the politics of the profession, the push for free-market reforms—all of it is happening in public education, too. Then we sat in on a breakout session covering recent changes to court mandates, and among a bunch of stressed out educators asking both smart and smart-ass questions about how yet another flip-flop in expectations would shape their day jobs, we felt right at home.

Why teach? And why teach now? Hasn't anyone told you not to teach—and mentioned, by the way, that teaching is excruciatingly hard work and that you will never receive the pay or the community respect you will so richly deserve? Why do you persist? On my mind was my teacher, Bill Ayers, who opened his book *To Teach* (2010, p. 1) with those prompts. In classic Bill fashion, he broaches an answer by telling a little story with big meaning—this one about why he writes—confessing sheer egoism, aesthetic enthusiasm, historical impulse, and political purpose, and then drawing parallels between the urgency of teaching and writing in this particular moment, all before tacking back and forth from exploring the contested space of schools to revisiting his own journey in them. The more I thought of Bill, and the longer I listened to the teachers commiserate, the more curious I became about their stories. Why do correctional educators teach? Unlike teachers who work in traditional settings, correctional educators must learn—usually through trial by fire—to make the most of an environment where lockdowns, head counts, meetings with lawyers, hearings, and transfers between facilities regularly disrupt classroom instruction (Tolbert, 2002). And why do they teach now, when Americans tend to be more retributive than restorative in our approach to harm and healing? Hasn't someone told them not to teach in corrections—for either job security or intrinsic value—because correctional teachers are held in even lower public regard than the police? Why do they persist? Just as my heart began to bleed, I was yanked back to the room by shameless self-congratulations for saving inmates from themselves. Yuck.

If I meet one more Nice White Lady or another Superman swooping in to rescue the downtrodden, I am going to be sick. True, the familiar sketch of an incarcerated person in the United States as young, male, of color, and of few means is largely accurate (Glaze, 2010). But too many of us in education carry over into the classroom our own racialized baggage on what it means to teach such a student, quick to presume that we need to step in for absent or negligent families, to turn street dreams into proper (read: White, middle-class) values and behaviors, and to break cycles of generational poverty. When what we really need to do is check ourselves, consider the consequences and global alternatives to deficit thinking, and make more conscious choices for our practice. This was the message that my friend and I delivered during our workshop, which—judging by the comments and questions that we fielded during and after the session ended—seemed to have been surprisingly well received.

Saving, civilizing, socializing "others" is, historically, a central purpose of schools; but some of us don't teach to be heroes. Some teachers teach to push themselves and their students to examine matters that are important to them, to ask embarrassing questions about why things are the way they are, to analyze who wins and who loses in current arrangements, and to explore possibilities for changing things they don't like. And they don't do any of it out of arrogance, nor for the sake of their careers or making money. These folks teach as an act of love. Before you get warm and fuzzy, I should be clear that I'm not referring to love in a romantic or mystical sense, not as happenstance or something we feel, but rather as a choice, something we do. Whenever I need straight talk on love, I go to bell hooks (2001, 2002), who argues in her trilogy of books on the subject that love is an exercise of will. For hooks, love is the action a person takes to enhance, protect, or alter another's life on his or her terms. **To teach from a place of love, then, is to empower**—to open your eyes and see the strengths and struggles of the three-dimensional beings in front of you, and to fearlessly put your ass on the line to help somebody meet a fuller measure of his or her own humanity.

This is the kind of teacher the profession so urgently needs, the kind I hope my brother will find soon, that he didn't have before. Looking back, I can see specific windows of opportunity that nobody slung open. In high school, Chris was the kind of student who could easily fall through the cracks: smart as a whip and bored out of his mind, disengaged, spotty in attendance. My brother's grades weren't remarkable. He wasn't an athlete or a band geek or otherwise active in any extracurricular programs that may have connected him to the school in some meaningful way. So when he stopped going altogether, not a single school adult noticed—or, if anyone did, nobody seemed to care. No one called or stopped by the house to see what was up. Had my parents been asked, they would have likely shared the same tidbits I told you—that Chris had never quite properly healed from the school wounds he'd sustained back in 4th grade, that his curiosity and bounding energy had been mistaken for an inability to sit still and think straight, that with repetition he'd learned to believe this himself. They would have said that Chris had checked out of school long before he dropped out. No one asked Chris where he thought he was going, except for the counselor who documented my brother's "transfer" to another educational institution, rather than calling it what it was and counting it as a loss— an awfully common and commonly understood practice to protect institutional interests by manipulating the numbers. Had people expressed genuine concern, they'd have discovered that Chris was heading to the Job Corps and maybe impressed upon him that it was not a good idea at a time when there were no jobs. Oh, how I wish there had been someone from the school—a teacher, a counselor, a dean, a principal, a superintendent—to say to Chris: (1) Being in school is a lot safer for you than not, (2) you matter to me and to many other people here, and (3) we'll go to the depths to figure out why you want to leave and to keep you around. I refuse to believe it would have taken much more than that for this rotten story I am writing about my brother to be different.

★   ★   ★

In a clumsy attempt to break the ice with Chris, I had him to agree to play a game of 21 Questions, in which people get to know each other better by making up and asking each other 21 questions about anything they want. With all that reliving his last birthday had excavated for me—his impending legal fight, what he did and did not do to pass the time in jail, and the connections to his educational background—asking Chris to narrate his own memory from his 21st birthday was one of my first orders of business. Bursting my bubble, a swift and uncomplicated "I remember being drunk" immediately came up for him. "Ooooookay," I said, "moving right along."

We discussed his favorite color, his most desired superhuman power, his future kids' names, his preference for ice cream over cake, his favorite movie, his best buddies, and his inability to recall the last time he heard a good joke.

"What do you want to be when you grow up?" I asked. Chris began, "I don't want to be nothing really, no doctor or lawyer or nothing." Then he stretched his imagination and said, "Get a job in construction or behind a desk," and then he pushed himself further: "Be a rapper or a basketball player." Then he backtracked, saying, "Let's get serious. I'll do anything."

I asked him to describe himself in three words: He replied, "mysterious, unpredictable, and adventurous.

His strong suit? "The gift of the gab."

His greatest limitation? A weak vocabulary that limits his gift of the gab, and he added, a "lack of education. My 8-year-old niece knows more times tables than me."

Speaking of your niece, I probed, how would you explain your life to her and your nephews? Chris said: "When they are older, I'll tell them I went down the wrong path, and once you go down that path, it's hard to make a U-turn." He went on to say that, if he could, he'd use a few pieces of advice he didn't take before, such as being told to stay in school, go to college, and grow up slowly.

I wondered if he had any words of wisdom for me as I try to raise my own little boys into men, and after prefacing his comments with a compliment on how well I've done so far and with a reminder to take whatever he says with a grain of salt, he offered, "Be a cool parent, someone they feel comfortable talking to."

Chris knows I am uptight when it comes to my sons. I am obsessive about schooling, routines, strict limits on screens, research on rearing and educating African American males, and doing whatever I can to prepare them for flourishing lives. Language is another one of my sticking points, which means, among other things, that I correct anyone who calls Zachary or Logan by any name other than the one I filed with the government. Even something as inoffensive as "mama's boy," which Chris swears befits my oldest, encourages me to act the self-appointed sergeant-at-arms of tongue. "He is not a mama's boy," I insist, and then in a mockery of my real voice, Chris adds, "He's a people's person." That's right; I believe the old adage that we speak things into existence.

What Chris doesn't know—well, didn't know until the tables turned and his questions prompted me to tell—is that I am this way because of him. I carry my brother and my boys with me everywhere. The decisions I make as a sister and mom, the projects I choose to work on as a scholar, what and how I teach as a professor, how I function as a citizen—all of these are shaped by what I think I've seen. I am, after all, a firsthand witness to a strong flame being smothered.

Chris couldn't come up with 21 questions. He thought deeply as he constructed four. All four were uncomfortable and liberating prompts to react to, allowing me to communicate with Chris like I never have before, but one of his questions blew my mind. He asked me point-blank: "Why do you think I ended up like this?" By now, you know this is a knot I have been trying to untangle on the page and to bring to some resolution. But it wasn't until that moment, when he put me on the spot, that I realized I don't have it just yet—no definitive clarity on the causes and correlates; I'm not sure whether I will ever have *the* answer. What my digging has turned up are some credible hunches, possible directions, and more questions about what it means for young Black men to come of age these days. That is, in a nutshell, what I told Chris in a mumbling and fumbling kind of way, and it is, I think, all that any of us could honestly say.

CHAPTER 5

Walk the Path

FOLLOWING SOMEONE THROUGH the school-to-prison pipeline is like chasing a violent storm—fascinating, full of adventure, and scary as hell. Yet, even a storm can be predicted. Its magnitude can be measured. It can be observed from hundreds of miles away. The fact is you would be hard-pressed to name the school-to-prison pipeline as such, to call it like it is, until you have seen some unlucky soul reach its tragic end. I have named it and called it because I hate that I have seen it, but now what? What more can I do with this essay, especially when my plan for it to serve as a talking piece blew up in smoke?

I suppose a girl can dream. I can step away from the immediacy of the story and reflect on what it amounts to, what it makes me wonder. I can pretend to stand in an auditorium facing a big audience filled with many of the people who might benefit from hearing what I think—future teachers, brand-new and seasoned teachers, teacher educators, educational leaders, others who run schools, and of course, my own family, too. To complete the fantasy, let's say I have titled my comments "Getting Intimate: A Vision of Love, Justice, and Joy in Education." I will end, then, with a transcript of my brief, imagined address:

"GETTING INTIMATE: A VISION OF LOVE, JUSTICE, AND JOY IN EDUCATION"

Thank you. Thanks to the organizers of this important forum and thanks to all of you for being here to see it. Let me first acknowledge the familiar faces in the room—my colleagues and students from the university, my friends and comrades from across the city, my family sitting proudly in the front row. I want to give an exaggerated wink and nod to my baby brother, Chris, especially. It is really because of him that I have something to share with you today.

It is probably safe to say for most of these folks who know me and my work quite well that a certain level of compulsion and coercion brought them to this talk, but for the rest of this beautiful, bright-eyed audience, I can only assume that you showed up because of the title. "Getting Intimate"—what a sexy, provocative way to be lured into a serious reflection on the social contexts of education and contemporary schools. There are perhaps other titles that more appropriately define the current moment we are in. At a time of standardization, accountability, and corporate-style reform, when routine and detachment from the messiness of teaching and learning are the only surefire ways to keep your job and your sanity, certainly, "Getting Intimate" suggests a bold path forward. In the next 10 minutes or so, I am going to make a short pitch for why we should do it anyway, for why love, justice, and joy in education are dangerous and worthwhile pursuits. I have been told that after 10 minutes a bullhorn will politely signal the time for me to pass the microphone. So, I want to keep my remarks to those three quick points—love, justice, and joy. These are three concepts that better explain exactly what I mean when I suggest that we—teachers, teachers' teachers, administrators, and anyone else who cares deeply about the social and academic lives of young people—ought to consider letting a commitment to intimacy guide our work.

Point One: Love

To explore this first idea, I want to start out with a little experiment. When I say the word *love*, what comes to mind? [Audience member offers "something warm and fuzzy."] Something warm and fuzzy. [Audience member offers "funny, giddy feelings."] Okay, funny, giddy feelings. Anything else? [Audience member offers "romance."]

All of these are perfectly sensible descriptions of love, but, in my mind, love is something different. I take cues from others who argue that love is not an emotion or a feeling, but an action. Love is the action we take to enhance or alter our own or somebody else's well-being; love is what we do to make people happier and healthier. Right off the bat and without any deep theoretical discussion, **love seems inextricably connected to the world of education and schools, teaching and learning.**

★   ★   ★

Feminist scholar Beth Brant (1994) tells us, "Who we are is written on our bodies, our hearts, our souls," and that in each of us there is a desire to be known and felt, to be acknowledged and validated, and to have our histories confirmed—to be witnessed for "what has been and what is to be" (p. 74). Witnessing, as an act of love, involves a deliberate attendance to people, seeing and taking notice of that which they believe is meaningful. Fears and desires are situated in a sense of past and future, and experiences become the fabric of time and space. To witness is to validate the existence of stories, and to protect their places in the world. Becky Ropers-Huilman (1999) writes: "We are acting as witnesses when we participate in knowing and learning about others, engage within constructions of truth, and communicate what we have experienced to others" (p. 23). For Ropers-Huilman, witnessing is qualitatively different from simply observing or looking at people.

I am reminded of the 1990s flick *White Men Can't Jump* in which one of the main characters, Sidney, claims that his counterpart, Billy, can't possibly hear the rich messages and music of Jimi Hendrix. "Look, man," Sidney says, "you can listen to Jimi but you can't hear him. There's a difference, man. Just because you're listening to him doesn't mean you're hearing him."

We might make a similar distinction between watching and witnessing. When we show our love for others—our students and their families—by witnessing their lives, we are complicit in active and partial meaning-making about those experiences, up close and personal, brazenly in their business. It means that we want to know what pleases and interests them, what saddens and shuts them down, what they are curious about, what sets their souls on fire. **Although it is impossible to really know other people or to completely understand what is happening to them, the act of witnessing is an invitation to pay attention, to reflect, to learn about lived lives, and to explore rationalizations of people's experiences.**

There is a particular urgency for the act of witnessing within the context of marginalization or wrongdoing. Being a spectator of calamities taking place both near and far is a quintessential part of the modern experience. I think of the recurring theme in slave narratives and the writings of Holocaust survivors who describe the trauma of public indifference to their struggles—the persistent feeling of invisibility and being made mute—as equally egregious assaults. At a minimum, bearing witness to the pain of other people who are significant is the act of validating and advancing their fundamental rights to peace, fairness, and humanity.

We do this by watching closely in the particular contexts in which our people try to make sense of things. We listen intently and provide a captive audience for critical reflections on the tough questions of guilt and responsibility. Dori Laub (1992) warns, "the absence of an empathic listener, or more radically the absence of an addressable other, an other who can hear the anguish . . . and thus affirm and recognize their realness, annihilates the story" (p. 68). For Laub, and for me as well, the act of listening is vital to the production and co-ownership of people's truths. But it is also the obligation of engaging the conversation that is central to the process of getting intimate.

Engaging points us to the posing of problems and the highlighting of contradictions that are inherent to all experiences of the peopled world. To engage is to put people in deliberate dialogue around the mundane, the taken-for-granted, the whispered, and the hushed. When we engage, we publicly name what we have witnessed and draw upon multiple vantage points—including our own lenses and perspectives—for a fuller and more complicated understanding of people's issues. Through engaging, we aim to establish the conditions for personal empowerment. Patti Lather (1991) reminds us that this means we create the space for "analyzing ideas about the causes of powerlessness, recognizing systemic oppressive forces, and acting both individually and collectively to change the conditions of our lives" (p. 4). Of course, providing the opportunity for people to speak for themselves and with others may not, in fact, lead them to do so, but there is an obligation on the part of any educator who witnesses and engages loved ones' lives to take some course of action.

Some of you know that I recently wrote an essay about Chris—a short, accessible piece that tracks the winding train of my thoughts on his life. It is biographical and "memoir-like." It is not your typical academic text, and as terrific as my brother is, it ain't no hagiography, either. Chris is not shy about the fact that he's having a difficult time getting along these days, and that being a young Black man with a record of court involvement doesn't make for an abundance of open doors. Chris himself usually admits more than that. For the past several years, my brother has so often conceded to lying in a bed of his own making that I feel like he's hypnotized, and being the skeptic that I am, I find myself tempted to shake him and yell, "Wake up! It's not all your fault." But whose fault is it? How did a boy born to a nurturing, committed village of kinfolks end up fighting five felony cases? I can't claim to know the science behind that, but in the essay, I tried with all my might to sort through and retrace the steps that could have led him here. Every kid has a story of incalculable value. Each of us wants to be witnessed and engaged, and writing about my brother—and his horrible journey through the school-to-prison pipeline—was my attempt to do that. It was my course of action. My writing was a testimony—an incomplete account of events—a vehicle through which I came to know my brother, myself, and the pitfalls of my profession a bit better. That cognizance and willingness to open up to the possibilities of changing and being changed is what love in education is all about.

Jawanzaa Kunjufu has authored many books on the condition of African American males, the most popular being *Countering the Conspiracy to Destroy Black Boys* (2005). He is often considered a separatist, a man of many opinions and few credentials, but I think he raises some pretty good points. One is: **"You cannot teach a child you do not love. You cannot teach a child you do not respect. You cannot teach a child you do not understand"** (p. 184). This is, I think, one of the most critical elements necessary for the creation of safe and productive learning environments.

Point Two: Justice

I have to establish my credibility as a mother of two small boys and a teacher educator at a comprehensive university on the far south side of Chicago. Before that, I taught formerly incarcerated students who were returning to school to earn a high school diploma. And before that, I worked with youth in whatever way I could—as a mentor, a tutor, and a substitute teacher. All the while and in each of those capacities, I liked to see myself not only as a teacher, but as a teacher activist. That concept, too, carries particular meanings.

Intuitively, the phrase *teacher activist* conjures images of fist-pumping, community-organizing, card-carrying union folks. Being a teacher in Chicago, where there are plenty of educational issues to be moved by, I resonate with this vivid portrayal. Yet again, I see the term *teacher activist* as suggesting something in particular, something useful for our purposes of thinking through what "Getting Intimate" might mean and how it might look in our workspaces. Let me riff, parenthetically, on the concerns and contexts of teacher activists as a prelude to my second point on justice.

Schools in the United States historically serve certain public goals that teachers are instrumental in meeting: the political, which asks teachers to indoctrinate patriotic citizens and groom future leaders; the social, which asks teachers to foster responsible, independent, law-abiding community members; and the economic, which asks teachers to prepare young people for the labor force and the free market (Hinchey, 2008; Spring, 2008). Teacher activists, who are considered a special kind of teacher, go about achieving these goals in unique ways.

Foremost for teacher activists is educational reform that contributes to equity in outcomes for students, schools, and the wider community. This means that inside of the classroom, teacher activists push themselves and students "to examine matters of importance to them, to ask why things are the way they are, to analyze who benefits most from the status quo, and to explore possibilities for changing conditions they don't like" (Hinchey, 2008, pp. 122–123). Outside of the classroom, teacher activists rely upon a variety of methods and outlets to provoke dialogue for transformation, including writing, petitioning, rallying, demonstrating, volunteering, lobbying, and more. The strategy is to do what can be done within the confines of school buildings and to complement such work with educational efforts elsewhere. To understand this micro-macro approach to teaching and learning, it is helpful to know that teacher activists are unabashed skeptics. That is to say, they are intentional about identifying their own and others' assumptions, seeking alternatives and making conscious choices for their practice. It is also true that teacher activists seriously doubt the overarching narrative of schooling and education for a more democratic society; teacher activists support the ideal but recognize the current reality. In fact, what gives rise to teacher activism is the existence of glaring inequities, intolerance, exclusion, and otherwise marginalizing conditions.

Naturally, the idea of teachers as activists makes many people uncomfortable. Teachers may function in any of the familiar roles that are formally and informally assigned to them—as a mentor, a parent, a guide on the side, a sage on the stage, an advocate, a counselor—but, in the current era of standardization, accountability, and corporate-style schooling, the word *activist* is often understood as code for polemic. It is not uncommon for teacher activists to take flak from colleagues or supervisors for paying too much attention to what is going on outside of the classroom, presumably at the expense of what is going on inside it. To that critique, teacher activists might reply in recognition and defense of the crucial interplay between content and real-world context for teaching and authentic learning. Other stakeholders in the teaching profession—politicians and policymakers, for example—may claim that teacher activists proselytize; teacher activists are too radical, too political. To that concern, teacher activists would say something on the order of what Patricia Hinchey (2008) articulated: "there is no such thing as a politically neutral school; and, there is no such thing as a politically neutral teacher. The question is not *whether* particular ideologies are being promoted, but *which* ones are—and how well we like them" (p. 15).

Given these sociopolitical contexts, it is reasonable to wonder why teacher activists engage in this kind of work. My answer borrows from sociologist C. Wright Mills (2000): Teacher activists do not see a neat split between their work and their lives. They take both too seriously to allow such separation, and they want to use each for the enrichment of the other.

Teacher activists draw on a wide range of frameworks—multiculturalism, critical theories, theories of care, spirituality, love, multidimensional ethical theory, theories of participatory democracy, and anti-oppressive education—to make sense of and reconcile the duality. Dantley and Tillman (2010) capture many of these theoretical lenses with five specific characteristics that clarify the definition, application, and requirements of teachers as activists: (1) a consciousness of the broader social, cultural, and political contexts of schools; (2) the critique of the marginalizing behaviors and predispositions of schools and their leadership; (3) a commitment to the more genuine enactment of democratic principles in schools; (4) a moral obligation to articulate a counter-vision or narrative of hope regarding education; and (5) a determination to move from rhetoric to civil rights activism. What teacher activists are after is social justice.

Teacher activists might be considered what some call transformative or public intellectuals. Public intellectuals recognize the demanding labor of pushing back on institutions that help maintain the social, political, and economic status quo. They are compelled to engage these issues anyway on the basis of a particular principle that is assumed to be universal: "that all human beings are entitled to expect decent standards of behavior concerning freedom and justice from worldly powers or nations, and that deliberate or inadvertent violations of these standards need to be testified and fought against courageously" (Said, 1994, pp. 11–12). There are no hard and fast rules to follow in expressing this commitment—in either overt or less recognizable ways. But as public intellectuals, teacher activists take on a responsibility "to raise embarrassing questions, to confront orthodoxy and dogma (rather than to produce them), to be someone who cannot easily be co-opted by governments or corporations, and whose raison d'etre is to represent all those people and issues that are routinely forgotten or swept under the rug" (Said, 1994, p. 12). At the bottom of this is a recognition that education can and should be for enlightenment and liberation.

However *activism* is defined, in order for teachers to meaningfully ground their work in activism, certain resources are necessary. Marshall and Oliva (2010) argue that teachers "need strategies, revolutionary ones in some contexts, for rethinking and taking leadership for social practices to better meet diverse students' needs. Also educators need the language to translate intellectual contexts into practice and experiential understandings. They need guidance, encouragement, examples, and support to practice leading discussions with community groups and politicians" (p. 4). They also need scholarship, large bodies of interdisciplinary research, to lean on for sustenance and perspective.

Point Three: Joy

I am running out of time, so I'll keep this point direct: All of us tend to get so caught up in the bullshit of our work that we forget that education is the most terrific, impactful, interdisciplinary profession there is. **We forget that our job is to give students—the teachers, philosophers, doctors, scientists, attorneys, firefighters, and more of the future—an education that is responsive to their identity and cultural backgrounds.**

In my backpack, I usually carry a copy of Leif Gustavson's *Youth Learning on Their Own Terms* (2007) as a constant reminder. In this book, Gustavson articulates a vision of youth-orientated learning environments, classrooms in particular, that tap into the important work that young people produce outside of school. This vision is informed by Gustavson's reflections on his own experiences with students as a middle school teacher and the ethnographies he produced in collaboration with three teenagers (two of whom are his former students): Ian, a zine writer; Gil, a turntablist; and Miguel, a graffiti artist. Through their stories, Gustavson pushes back on the framing of school buildings as the only places to acquire knowledge and highlights instead the ways in which youth construct knowledge through interaction with a variety of domains, people, and media. He argues that teachers needs to be attuned to the ways youth build communities of practice and also how youth are "reflective, experimental, performative, evaluative, and interpretive when considering how the practice of teaching can be informed by what constitutes a rigorous and meaningful learning environment" (Gustavson, 2007, p. 15).

I wish Gustavson's book had been written many years ago. If my brother Chris had read it, then perhaps it would have validated his sense that school was too often an uneasy and uncomfortable place for him to be, not because he didn't fit in, but because the learning environment did not incorporate his skills and his personal ways of exploring things. If my family had read it, we might not have looked at Chris' penchant for songwriting and music production as hobbies, but as windows into understanding him. If his teachers had read it, they might have designed learning spaces that encouraged him to stay in school and out of trouble. Gustavson's ideas are worth noting in extensive detail.

Gustavson offers two interconnected ways in which teachers can create productive learning spaces: as ethnographers and amateurs in their classrooms and also as conscious designers of the learning experience. Quickly, Gustavson (2007) explains ethnography in order to help readers understand what the work of a teacher-ethnographer entails:

Ethnographers approach their phenomena realizing that they know little and that the people who are part of the phenomena, the "natives," know a lot. With this realization, ethnographers position themselves as the learners and the people who are part of the phenomena as the teachers. They *observe, interview, and participate* in order to better understand the people whom they are studying. When we make this analogous to teaching, it is our job as teachers to figure out how our students are mathematicians, historians, writers, and scientists *in their lives*, instead of assuming that they are not or that they need to be taught how to be. Teacher-ethnographers collect bits of youth conversation, notes thrown out in the trash, and other kinds of artifacts. They recognize dress, musical tastes, and cultural movements. Teacher-ethnographers use these data to not only inform them in terms of who the youth are as people but to also inform their understanding of how the ways youth work and learn in their worlds are ways into being mathematicians, historians, scientists, and writers. Therefore, a teacher who is influenced by ethnographic practices would no longer look at . . . [Chris, for example, and his interest in songwriting and music production] as simply a product. Instead, the teacher would recognize that . . . [Chris] is involved in a practice—habits of mind and body—that enables him to do the work of a writer. (p. 138, emphasis in original)

Gustavson writes that the teacher-ethnographer knows it is part of his or her job to understand the how and why of students' creative practices because it is one of the ways in which youth make meaning. A teacher who takes an ethnographic stance finds ways to understand the depth and complexity of Chris' songwriting and music production, for example, or works to see how Chris is reflective, experimental, and evaluative in the manner in which he works in his own ways. Gustavson (2007) channels the writing of John Dewey to describe the "experience" into which teacher-ethnographers tap:

Dewey argues that one's learning is influenced by both outside and inside forces. He refers to these outside forces as "persons and things." The persons and things that youth interact with are in part influenced by what the youth have experienced in their pasts. These past people and things influence present people and things, which shape future experiences. Instead of taking this truism for granted, as Dewey suggests many do, he pushes us to look into the "human activities" of youth for their "educational import." In other words, the everyday experiences of youth are sophisticated, meaningful, and not unlike the knowledge teachers expect students to develop in schools. . . . Dewey suggests that if we tune our teaching practice to these habits, we will avoid the pitfalls of imposing learning on students. This imposition has many deleterious results. On the one hand, students may eventually drop out because of sheer boredom. On the other, those who choose to stay will develop learning habits that do not prepare them to be mathematicians, historians, writers, and scientists. (p. 139)

I don't want to get too bogged down in philosophy, but understanding youth cultural practices as an ethnographer assumes that youth are inherently creative problem-posers and problem-solvers, and that they already have some special knowledge of a discipline. Gustavson insists that understanding youth cultural practices as ethnographers requires teachers to be "amateurs" in the way that Edward Said envisioned: someone who is not bound by a particular approach to problems or ideas. An amateur works with students through a problem that stems from those students' creative practices. For example, a history teacher would be concerned with teaching students how to trouble historical "facts," but would connect it to the practices of songwriting and entertain powerful tangential talk rooted in everyday life. Rather than focusing on the end itself, an amateur would be aware of the educative process—the daily habits of mind and body—that forge the construction of knowledge.

Remember Kunjufu? Love, mutual respect, and understanding are the work of amateurs:

Said defines amateurism as "an activity that is fueled by care and affection rather than by profit and selfish, narrow specialization." . . . Teachers can see their students as allies in a common project. They expect to learn from their students, not just how to be better teachers or how to understand fractions in a new way but also about the world in general. Said writes that teachers as amateurs "can enter and transform the merely professional routine most of us go through into something much more lively and radical; instead of doing what one is supposed to do one can ask why one does it, who benefits from it, how can it reconnect with a personal project and original thoughts." . . . Teachers who see themselves as amateurs value students' experiences in creative practices as resources for their own understanding of academic subject knowledge in particular and the world more broadly. (Gustavson, 2007, p. 141)

Once a teacher sees him/herself as an ethnographer/amateur and his/her role as, in part, developing a way of being in the classroom, rather than a set of things to do with students for class period or school day, then he/she can begin to translate that understanding into designing a youth-oriented learning space. Such an environment utilizes the technical skills and conceptual knowledge that students gain through their creative practices. This does not mean that Chris would haul his equipment to school and lay tracks in class. Instead, Gustavson (2007) says, he "should be encouraged to use the habits of mind and body that are a part of these crafts to do the work of the class" (p. 143). He should perceive that his ways of learning on his own terms are valued and essential. Gustavson lays out how teachers can implement various forms of performance, experimentation, reflection, evaluation, interpretation, and communities of practice into their classroom design as ways of creating spaces for kids like Chris to work and learn in a productive environment.

Besides end-of-unit culminations, for example, teachers can offer more informal types of performance where students can try their work out, in mid-production, as Chris so often does with his songwriting and music production. Gustavson (2007) writes that these informal performances "provide essential feedback from peers in order to determine where to go next or even if it is worth proceeding with the project at all. They also open up avenues for critical conversation about the craft itself and the meaning of the products being constructed. . . . Multiple forms of performance create authentic reasons for students to experiment further, reflect on their work, evaluate its efficacy, and interpret audience reactions" (p.

144). Performing widely provides students the chance to identify multiple audiences for their work within and outside of classrooms or schools. *Experimentation, Reflection, Evaluation, Interpretation.* Testing out, reflecting on, and evaluating ideas within their creative practices is an important part of performance. Experimentation opens up new possibilities for their work, and helps them see what they are capable of and how they can build on it. *Communities of Practice.* Teachers and students must articulate to one another and to themselves how they work. Gustavson (2007) suggests that this kind of ongoing conversation builds "a database or repertoire of authentic tactics and strategies for doing the work of the class that comes from the ways in which youth work in the world and from the ways in which established historians, scientists, mathematicians, and writers engage in their respective crafts" (p. 149). This connects the ways in which youth make meaning with the way that professionals do their work, helping youth see how they are budding professionals. Teachers must also work alongside students to develop a sense of shared learning, as students would do with others in their communities of practice.

Gustavson focuses intensely on teachers in traditional classrooms, but the same ideas hold true for educators in alternative placements and other learning environments, such as a young person's home. **This is probably more than you ever wanted to know about Gustavson (and maybe even about Chris), but what both make clear is that any safe and productive learning space is one in which every student is valued and encouraged to explore, learn, and work in his or her own ways. And oh, what a joy this brings!**

What I am trying to grapple with are the guiding principles of what I think of as the intimate labor in which educators can and should engage. Getting intimate means giving a damn, worrying about what happens to people in our everyday lives. It means attending to their individual needs, perspectives, and interests—by asking the basic questions: who, what, where, when, why, and how. It means accepting that the answers to these questions may bring an uneasy and jarring level of consciousness to the ways in which we receive, recognize, and respond to others and ourselves. It means organizing our work around caring—for human affections, weaknesses, and anxieties—to get to know people in all of their particularity. And then, our challenge is to connect what we know with what we do. **Getting intimate means teaching and learning in the spirit of community and in solidarity, or as my mother once said, being willing to "walk the path" with youth.**

In the final analysis, getting intimate requires every adult who works with young folks in our education systems to love and respect children, to wake up each day to struggle and strive toward social justice, and to find joy and pleasure in it all, or to go do something else. Thank you.

Epilogue

WHENEVER I LEAF THROUGH the pages of this book and reread a passage here or there, I invariably wish for the belated editorial authority to make my brother's story seem sweeter than it really is. I want to add a dash of happy notes, smooth out some jagged edges, and sound a little nicer. I think of "When Keeping It Real Goes Wrong," a series of skits on the television sketch-comedy *Chappelle's Show* that satirizes the consequences of rattling off uninhibited, and suddenly feel a rush of nervous energy. But then a generous voice inside my head whispers that what I wrote is a personal essay, not a manifesto, and that for goodness sake, I need to let it be.

It is important to remember the personal essay doesn't promise that goodness will feel good, nor end neatly and well. Among its essential conditions are candor and sincerity, which mean that I didn't have to fluff the earlier chapters or what has happened with Chris in the months since I finished writing them: He moved out of our parents' house and, with their support, into a place of his own; he completed a construction job training program; he still sees a therapist and takes recovery a day at a time; he opened up to a loving relationship with a young woman and her toddler; and he closed the silly case of the missing jeans. One down; five more felony fights to wage. No need to embellish or stretch for positivity; I can just stick to the facts.

I must have started, stopped, and started this project again a hundred times before I fell into a literary tradition that would let me tell my version of things in an uncomplicated way. The personal essay, a kind of informal essay, is unbound by the scholarly conventions that tripped me up before: It is flexible in form and style; it embraces contradictions, confessions, and situations that can't be easily explained; and it is united by the scandalous letter "I." Read the work of contemporary essayists—Joan Didion, Adrienne Rich, Vivian Gornick, Phillip Lopate, Gayle Pemberton, Scott Russell Sanders, Sara Suleri— and see the first-person singular portray the particulars of character and voice unlike any other word. See, as well, the conversational element that distinguishes the technique of the personal essay. Phillip Lopate notes in *The Art of the Personal Essay* (1995), "The writer seems to be speaking directly into your ear, confiding everything from gossip to wisdom," telling about herself and, to some degree, about us all. "Through sharing thoughts, memories, desires, complaints, and whimsies, the personal essayist sets up a relationship with the reader, a dialogue—a friendship, if you will, based on identification, understanding, testiness, and companionship" (p. xxiii).

Are we there yet? I sure hope so. I didn't tell my brother's business, bare my naked soul, and allow you to eavesdrop on the uncertainties of my curious mind for nothing.

It was in graduate school when creative nonfiction first appealed to me as a mode of inquiry and I began writing academic papers about Chris in the genre. Once, I remember describing to my classmates in a Research Methods course the central questions upon which this book was ultimately crafted, and proposing the thorny process of exploring them through narrative. My professor—a respected, prolific scholar in the field—asked, "How will this project move beyond navel-gazing?" He went on to say, "I mean, no one will base policy decisions on your brother." Message across—thanks, pal!

I am not so naïve as to believe that personal narrative is a vanguard methodology. Though there is a long line of studies by researchers of their own communities—over 3 decades' worth of publications—I am well aware that this kind of writing is still up and coming. You see, academics have a hard time dealing with the place of intimacy, closeness, and relationships in scholarly work. Even in education, which is so fundamentally driven by what people believe, feel, and do, stories—simple, singular stories about these things—are often underprivileged forms of insight. Part of the trouble is that we lack gold standards and "best practices" on how to navigate the procedural and ethical messiness of life experiences. The more substantial barrier is our tendency to think about "research" not as a careful examination of specific social, intellectual, or political problems that bear on real people, but as the product of observable and replicable processes, of science.

Now, as it has for the last 50 years, positivistic conceptions of science have dominated education discourse and divided the research community along predictable lines of epistemological and methodological approach: Quantitative camps of scholars, with their emphasis on the separation of truth and values in the interest of objectivity are pitted against their more "touchy-feely" colleagues, many of whom use a range of exploratory and qualitative methods. A case in point is what education philosopher Kenneth Howe (2009) calls the "new scientific orthodoxy" in education research, "which has been codified in the National Research Council's (NRC) *Scientific Research in Education* (2002) and reinforced in its subsequent *Advancing Scientific Research in Education* (2004) as well as in the American Educational Research Association's (AERA) *Standards for Reporting on Empirical Social Science Research in AERA Publications* (2006)" (p. 428). The authors of each of these reports articulated and promoted a cohesive framework for scientific inquiry in education that distinguishes "research" from other kinds of intellectual pursuits and summarily excludes "challenges and alternative views from the conversation about education policy and practice" (Howe, 2009, p. 437).

If the exclusionary effect is an unintended consequence of explicating scholarly norms internal to the education research community, it is also a fiscally responsible consideration of external factors. Purging the education enterprise of "(so-called) research that consists of some combination of subjective, ungeneralizable, partisan, hypercritical, incomprehensible, useless, speculative conjecturing" (Howe, 2009, p. 438) in order to claim the mantle of science provides "a means for education research to retain or enhance [prestige, credibility] support—including financial, from its patrons, such as the federal government and private foundations" (Howe, 2009, p. 433). Within this context, embracing personal narrative in education research is beyond suspect; it is bad for business.

The implications of such thinking are far-reaching, as the space and tolerance for social inquiry that is committed to documenting the nuances of human lives, oppression, and resistance shrinks, and the risk of silencing, invisibility, and unemployment strengthens pressures to assimilate to dominant expectations of researcher practices. Ethnographer Harry Wolcott (2002) puts the point pithily: "If you don't do or present research as our self-appointed standard-bearers feel it should be done or presented, they [your colleagues] may do *you* in" (p. 167).

Personal narrative researchers in the academy are poised to reconcile a kind of duality akin to W.E.B. DuBois' "double-consciousness" (1990), in which Blacks in the United States at the turn of the 19th century were compelled, he argued, to preserve perspectives as both Africans and simultaneously as Americans. We are at once committed to developing research processes that are more ethical, sympathetic, collaborative, useful, and connected to "real" lives, and at the same time, I think, struggling to maintain productive "academic" lives in the interest of legitimacy, collegial respect, and professional marketability. It is an inconvenient duplicity, a path fraught with contradiction and conflict that leads to self-doubt—of our autobiographies, intentions, and our own intuitive sense about what counts, who matters, and what questions are worth asking. Too often, scholars negotiate this tension by relegating themselves to prefaces and footnotes, or downplaying the controversial features of their work in their writing and speaking engagements. The flip side of what indigenous researcher Stephanie Daza (2008) refers to as "covering"—the ways in which we go about fitting in or playing roles in order to be perceived as legitimate scholars—is "preaching to the choir," circulating critical and innovative work within the safety of polite company. Meanwhile, the people whose lives our research is meant to shape bear the imprint of our politics.

Many scholars may not be certain of exactly *how* to embrace the personal in academic research or they may have ideas about how but choose not to *do* so. To suggest, however, that there are not ways in which we *can* bring the personal into our scholarly pursuits is a wicked idea. Having been professionally socialized to believe otherwise, I can assure you that nay-saying is a familiar trope.

I want to noodle on my dearest professor for a short while longer, not the bit about navel-gazing (which, by the way, I have put on my list of things to never utter to my own students) but about the scary claim that policymakers won't be sufficiently moved by my brother's story to make any notable changes that may shape his or other young people's lives. What was this about? The easiest possibilities to rule out are (1) that my professor underestimated the big implications of the small details in Chris' narrative and (2) that he was just being mean; back then, I had more ideas in my head than on the page, and so this generally affable guy didn't have much written material to misjudge. I also seriously doubt that my professor questioned the validity and reliability of using Chris as an informant; as an educational historian whose research subjects are mostly dead, I assume that my professor has a wide methodological imagination.

Many more people may legitimately ask why I chose to write about my brother rather than some other subaltern spirit, and the answer is simple: I have grown up with my brother, and his life is intricately linked to mine. I have long been interested in studying the experiences of Black boys who leave schools without a diploma, but I was *invested* in better understanding how my own kin had come to that place—as the old expression goes, "Blood is thicker than water."

Because each of us has our own story, another more complex concern might be explicating what makes *Chris'* story so special— "Why *him*?" My brother himself has repeatedly posed this question, and here I have printed a quick summation of the response that I have rehearsed with him: His story is chock-full of tensions and conflict about the hope and struggle of the educational arena, and about schools as spaces where questions of identity and justice are worked through. His story is about marginality and resistance, estrangement and resilience. His personal story pushes back on our public chatter around "bad" kids and their "dysfunctional" families. His story clearly points to moments and experiences that masked the opportunities of others. His story is both common and commonly misunderstood, and is given weight by its social, political, and historical contexts. In short, his story is critical to grappling with the very meaning of education and schooling. His story matters to people in the field.

Nobody schooled in qualitative research will be shocked to find out that I assume people, especially young people, are active thinkers, movers, and shakers of the world, and that each of us has the capacity to make sense of our experiences, to claim expertise on our own lives. I truly believe that my brother and other young people have the ability to tune adults in, to direct our gaze, and to move us toward a more just and humane world—if only we would delve close to the source of our quandaries, ask the simplest questions, and pay scrupulous attention to what they think we are up to. This book about my brother's story joins what has become a wide shelf of materials devoted specifically to the strength of youth voices.

Yet another familiar question is, "Why *just* him?" The notorious issue of sampling, and the authority of an "n" of one person, might be best understood through an illustrative example.

In the summer of 2009, investigative reporter Rex Huppke heard the story of 11-year old Devon Mallard. Devon was a student at Ray Elementary School in Chicago's Hyde Park community. Devon's academic and behavior troubles had gone back several years, and the Chicago Public Schools had not met his needs. At the end of Devon's 2nd-grade year, in 2005, a teacher's assessment showed that he was performing at a kindergarten level, and although he was never fully evaluated or provided with any special services, he was identified as having a learning disability. He wasn't found eligible for special education classes until January 2007, but by the time an Individualized Education Plan was created, Devon's reading scores had decreased and his behavior problems seemed to worsen. In September 2007, Devon's doctor diagnosed him with anxiety disorder, dyslexia, and oppositional defiant disorder, but his educational plan was not amended to reflect these disabilities. In August 2008, Shnette Tyler, the boy's mother, sought legal counsel and filed her first due-process complaint. In March 2009, an independent hearing officer ordered Chicago Public Schools to set up a proper education plan within 45 days, and to provide Devon with an array of weekly services, including psychological counseling, occupational therapy, and a reading tutor. Another 5 months later and nearing the start of his 6th-grade year, nothing had been done.

Huppke started asking around. He located Devon's mother, who was awaiting another administrative hearing to compel the school district to meet its obligations. "I'm just trying to get my son a good education, get him in a place where he can learn," she told Huppke. Huppke obtained court documents that chronicled Devon's history of learning disabilities and the absence of Chicago Public Schools' legal representation at two meetings that were scheduled to draft and finalize a new education plan. An outreach coordinator for Access Living, a disability rights group, told Ruppke what others suspected: Chicago Public Schools often "feel like they can push the limits and don't have to follow the letter of the law" in providing services for disabled youths. "They're doing this in case after case after case," Michael O'Connor, one of Devon's attorneys, said. Huppke caught up with Monique Bond, a school district spokeswoman, who would not discuss the specifics of Devon's case: "We are concerned any time the system has failed to meet the needs of a student," she said. "We're going to comply with the order." With the first day of school fast approaching, Devon's mother described to Ruppke the tough decision that she was grappling with: "Send him back to a school environment that has both failed and frustrated him or pull him out of school and let the legal system run its course." For Devon himself, the choice was a simple. "I don't want to be in that classroom," he said.

In August 2009, Ruppke published the story in the *Chicago Tribune*, along with an oversized, full-color photo of Devon, his innocent brown face sharper in the screen of the cellphone that he used to take his own picture than in the blur of the image taken by the paper's photographer. It was a subtle play in support of the article—intended to help us see Devon more vividly, clearly, up close and personal. Ruppke titled the report "1 Child Left Behind."

Printed on the newspaper's front page after 4 years of academic failure and two due-process complaints, that story got results. Following the report, Chicago Public Schools launched an internal review of its Office of Specialized Services, and the district began working with Devon's family and its attorneys to make sure the terms of the court order were met. "With Devon's case, whatever happened, we need to understand it so that it doesn't happen again," district spokeswoman Monique Bond told Ruppke. She said the district would look into how parents' due-process complaints are handled and make it "as expeditious as possible." A settlement was reached in October 2009, and though the family can't discuss it, Ruppke reported that Devon's mother said that for now she is happy with the outcome: Devon returned to classes and he is doing well.

This is the power of one—one investigator, one article, and one child to focus our attention on educational problems of critical proportions, to reveal the conditions under which some youth struggle to learn, and to hold people accountable. It is one way to help people who live, learn, and work alongside the country's Devons to see them, notice them, tap into fundamental understandings of humanity and justice. It is one compelling reason for each of us to ask, "What if this was my own kid?" Each story teaches important life lessons, and each story can extend and enrich our sense of the value of paying closer attention to people.

I am thinking of sociologist Clifford Shaw's *The Jack-Roller: A Delinquent Boy's Own Story* (1966), anthropologist Harry Wolcott's "Adequate Schools and Inadequate Education: The Life History of a Sneaky Kid" (1983), journalist Danny Lyon's *Like a Thief's Dream* (2007), and cultural critic Susan Sheehan's *Life for Me Ain't Been No Crystal Stair: One Family's Passage Through the Child Welfare System* (1993). These works vary in purpose, writing style, and research tradition, but each focuses on ascertaining the point of view of a single person, nestling the individual's perspective within broader contexts and rendering it chronologically on the basis, at least in part, of the words and writings of the participants themselves. Scholars who produce oral and life histories seem to understand this best. I lean on the purposes and standards of these folks' single-subject studies to work through and to defend my own.

But never mind me; the idea that a story or the mobilization of a bunch of stories is futile flies in the face of everything we know about the history of social movements in the United States. The Labor Movement, the Women's Movement, the Civil Rights Movement, the Student Movement, the LGBT Movement, the movement to Occupy Wall Street—all of these social transformations and the legislation they inspired were sparked and carried on at particular moments by tales of unrest, resistance, and desire that were somehow documented and shared widely. A more recent and relevant example of policy decisions being made, at least partly, on the basis of stories can be seen in the Obama administration's responses to grassroots activism urging school adults to rethink discipline. The 2011 Supportive School Discipline Initiative, the first-ever 2012 Senate hearing on the school-to-prison pipeline, and the 2014 release of the federal School Discipline Guidance package were made possible because legislators got acquainted with maddening testimonies of school pushout.

At the end of the day, I see *Being Bad* as another accessible resource for people with the power of the pen. I will remember I wrote that here at the end of the book the next time I flip through it and a brief bout of panic ensues.

Afterword

Our prison nation—a plank in what historian Saidiya Hartman has termed the "afterlife of slavery"—is at a critical juncture. People across the country are asking with urgency the question Angela Davis posed in 2003: *Are Prisons Obsolete?* Shuttering prisons, repealing drug laws—once unthinkable, outrageous—are now championed by political actors from Attorney General Eric Holder to Republican Newt Gingrich. Even the *New York Times*, an institution some have argued has been entirely complicit in its intense promotion and advocacy of harsh sentencing, acknowledged the need for an "end to mass incarceration" in a May 2014 editorial. Perhaps not abolitionists, but we are all prison reformers now, or so it seems.

Yet this moment of restructuring requires careful attention. As schools and (some) prisons—public institutions that enclose Black and Brown people—close, what forms of capture emerge? Anticipating and resisting evolving patterns of enclosure requires a rigorous understanding of our current political moment. Beyond statistics and surveys, data sets and opinion polls, we need meticulous and grounded engagements with people's lives. And, as some seek to question a system that was working precisely as designed, how is the liberation of the millions enmeshed in and struggling to resist forms of civil and physical death recognized and prioritized?

Dr. Crystal Laura's *Being Bad* deftly chronicles her brother's punishing topography of schooling, and the collateral impacts of the acquisition of all the Chrises by our prison nation. While refused the status of research by her university's Institutional Review Board, a badge of honor I'd argue, Dr. Laura's voice also reminds us, particularly those working within the field of education, about the most powerful tool available for the *labor* of social change.

In 1994, reflecting on the *The Bluest Eye*, published in 1970, Toni Morrison expresses misgivings about how the novel's form, "to break the narrative into parts," and to center "the weight of the novel's inquiry on so delicate and vulnerable a character" could adequately negotiate the story's intertwined themes: slavery, White supremacy, misogyny, and poverty. She writes that "it didn't work: many readers remain touched but not moved."

For many, fragmentation is a valuable metaphor for how trauma shapes lives, yet Toni Morrison worries her form was too risky and dilutes the politics. Maybe a more conventional telling, more rule following, would move audiences? *Being Bad* reminds us otherwise. Yes, stories that boldly take on the beautiful awfulness of life—what many must forget or try to stuff into suitcases—are staggeringly risky. But unlike Morrison's equation, whether people are touched or moved is not solely the author's domain, and the truth's awful beauty makes the telling imperative and demands new forms. Beyond a win–lose scenario, the best tools to build the world we know we need are our bones and blood, our hands and hearts.

Telling the truth outside of conventional and accepted formats is risky. Unlike Dr. Laura, some might not be brave enough or ready to wade through. Others will be exhausted, no better for the telling, or even harmed by the violence of asking those willfully ignorant to listen. And everyday people's pain is repackaged as a redemptive story obscuring punishing histories and structural forces: bad kids done good. Or reworked as "character education": *Poor? Why didn't you pull yourself up by the bootstraps!*

These risks, and many more, are real. And yet as the poet and activist Muriel Rukeyser wrote in 1968: "What would happen if one woman told the truth about her life? The world would split open." With work, art, and our very lives this truth-telling must be done. Louder. Again. Truths move people to love the unsayable, to stay awake all night, or to see ourselves and the world, otherwise.

Splitting the world open demands new forms. Readers might pull messages other than those we desire from our work. This is a risk. But one that must be taken.

Truths that crack worlds remind audiences of the work to be done. With too many Chrises within the grasp of the prison nation, withering in special education classes and in-school detention halls; with mothers and lovers and sisters, like Crystal, waiting in lines from Riker's Island to San Quentin—what are our tasks? How will we move? Who will we move? What will we do now that this book is closed, but the lives and the labors unfinished? *Being Bad* splits us open. It is our work to take this political moment as our struggle and ensure that no one is left behind.

—Erica R. Meiners

On the Methods and Ethics of Intimate Inquiry

On the first page of this book, I noted that it was written for me and deliberately published with Teachers College Press for someone like you. In my mind, you are a scholar, a community organizer, a youth, a youth worker, a college student, a teacher or school administrator, a direct-service practitioner, a policymaker, a parent, or someone else who cares deeply about the social and academic worlds of Black boys. You belong to a niche of smart people in the world of education and schools who desperately want to understand what the school-to-prison pipeline looks like on the ground, people who want to study up and act out, people who seek methodological intervention in the field of education, and people who need to be in the know and on guard for the subtleties of these important problems. You read as widely and deeply as a hectic schedule will allow. You are a kind of writer, too, yes? Convoluted jargon drives you nuts, excessive length and distant writing styles put you to sleep, and all you want from a text is resonance, particularly when it is established through everyday language or an interesting story.

I want to tell another one: the story behind the story, which is about the particulars of how I constructed *Being Bad* and dealt with the many practical and ethical dilemmas it has raised. It seems to me that transparency about such things is important, though I realize that this part of the book is probably not for everyone. Those drawn to personal writing—in admiration, curiosity, distrust, or all three—will find the rest of Appendix A especially helpful. Others may want to fast-forward to Appendix B or stop reading altogether while the timbre of the earlier chapters is still abuzz.

THE LONG AND SHORT OF IT

This book was inspired by the doctoral dissertation that my dearest professor shot down and I stubbornly went through with anyway. Let me jog your memory: It was 2008. My grandparents had died. My parents were in therapy. I practically lived back home with my family as we reeled ourselves in from the precipice of insanity. On top of all of this, my teenage brother announced his plans to drop out of school. That was the sheer force of the moment when I cared more about wrapping my head around all of this and less about getting institutional permission to do it. Much like this essay, the dissertation fulfills at least two purposes:

1. It maps my family culling together and sometimes falling apart in attempt to better understand and help Chris.
2. It renders Chris visible and documents his social and academic marginality in a text to be read by an audience of educators.

I completed the dissertation early in 2011, but it ends with events that occurred in 2010. Back then, there simply was not enough space separating me from the hurt of Chris' first stint in Cook County Jail to write about it and the downward spiral that followed. *Being Bad* picks up where the dissertation left off with newfound courage and a fresh perspective.

In between the dissertation and the book, I received an award for my contribution to qualitative research from the American Educational Research Association, the largest professional organization in my field. Qualitative researchers are known to take on writing projects that seek to understand the meanings that actors make in situations, and to use themselves as instruments in the process. My work falls on the bohemian end of the spectrum of qualitative methodologies, closer to the artists and activists than to the straight-up academics, which is why I was pleasantly surprised to be recognized by the mainstream. I remember prancing away from the podium at the awards ceremony, clicking stilettos that had nothing on the high I was experiencing. I had delivered a spontaneous and funny and heartfelt acceptance speech, thanked all of the important people in my life. I had another sharp line on my resume. I was $500 richer. My name was in circulation among a wider community of scholars. And my mentor, my husband, and my son—decked out in a tuxedo-printed romper—were there to help me savor that fleeting moment. I schmoozed and took a few business cards, then floated back to my hotel room in something of a blur.

How did I pull it off? Graduate students often ask me about this, hoping to collect some tried-and-true tips to inform their own personal writing. Writing a dissertation is hard; writing autobiographical content into a dissertation is like getting blood from a stone, and honestly, I don't have any prescriptions. It seems to me that I was driven as much by intention as intuition.

I tried out two variations of the award-winning paper before settling on what to me felt right. Each of the three versions of my dissertation was rooted in a qualitative approach, and each raised questions about the necessity of new methodological and academic interventions in people's lives, and grappled with the politics of personal work within academic arenas. What differentiated the studies were the methods and ethics that I attended to, the kinds of dilemmas and possibilities that each version implied, and the progression with which I repositioned my brother at the forefront.

Variation One—Covering: A Study of Assimilation

Given my explicit research purposes, writing my brother out of the story appears to have been a visceral reaction. At the time, of course, realigning my dissertation with common notions of legitimate qualitative research felt like the most reasonable methodological decision to make. In March 2008, I first considered ditching altogether the idea of examining my brother's experiences. Instead, I thought it might be easier to redevelop on a larger scale an exploratory study that I had completed 5 months earlier for the purposes of a research methods course in which I was enrolled. I designed the pilot study to create dialogue within a Chicago public high school where I had previously worked around its policies and procedures related to student climate. The school's discipline policy and the juxtaposition of administrators' goals with student perceptions of the policy's meaning were of particular interest. The three-tiered system of behavior management, euphemistically referenced as the "Incentive Program," sorted the student body into colored groups: Gold Group, Red Group, and Orange Group. Membership in one group garnered a different set of rewards or penalties as opposed to belonging to the others. All students began each term in affiliation with the Red (default) Group. Then, depending on whether or not detentions were accumulated and served at the end of each school week, students could be moved between groups throughout the year. Belonging to the Orange Group, the bottom rung of the hierarchy, brought notable consequences: These students could not receive passes out of class, were required to display an orange identification card on their person, could not enter the dining hall during mealtime until all Gold and Red Group students had made their selections, and could not participate in extracurricular activities. Connection with the Orange Group carried, as well, significant ideological connotations: Students and staff alike recognized members of the Orange Group as the "bad kids."

I learned about the discipline policy during my tenure as a tutor for the school's college readiness program, but I had real reservations about engaging its politics. For one thing, I saw the Incentive Program as particularly problematic—a deliberate effort to monitor, sort, and contain troublesome Black adolescents who "are discursively constructed as under-achieving, violent-prone, education-aversive youth (i.e., the dregs of society, who are in need of discipline and restraint), [and] the imposition and presence of enforcement policies [as an effort] to 'civilize their untamed spirits'" (Brown, 2003, p. 126). I was also hesitant to support the policy because so many of the Orange Group students were my students, a relationship that enabled me to closely observe the stigma attached to membership in the group and the students' varying reactions to it. I cringed every time students seemed to play into others' expectations of "bad kids" or when students self-segregated, assuming that behavior problems proved intellectual inaptitude and apathy. I celebrated when I witnessed moments of resistance to these meanings. At some point, it occurred to me that I cared about them because, in circumstances and physical characteristics, they reminded me so much of my brother. Within a few short months, I left the job on good terms to pursue with vigor the roots of my intellectual curiosities that these young people managed to clarify for me.

I returned to the school shortly thereafter to satisfy the mutual interests that the principal and I shared: The principal sought feedback on the Incentive Program that would inform the school's improvement plan, and I wanted to fulfill the fieldwork requirement for my methods course on a topic of genuine interest and significance. I constructed, with much help from the principal, an interpretive study that helped us both understand the meaning that the Incentive Program had for students, and especially their thoughts about the Orange Group. I used notes that I jotted about my own observations and information shared during separate semi-structured interviews with the assistant principal, who created the discipline system, and one Orange Group student, and a questionnaire completed by 78 students to find out their impressions of the Incentive Program and the Orange Group. The study found that while students understood the official goals of the discipline policy, as articulated by the administrative staff and widely distributed written materials, they believed that an unofficial agenda was at work. Specifically, in contrast to the administrative perspective of the Incentive Program as a means of forging accountability and responsibility, maintaining order and consistency, and discouraging students from displaying behaviors that garnered detentions, students believed the policy to be racially discriminatory and damaging to their social and academic prospects.

Together with a classmate who helped with data analysis, I wrote the final report in language that would jibe with an audience of both my peers, who practiced traditional qualitative research techniques, and the school's administrative team. The presentation of my pilot study to the methods class received positive reactions, and seemed to move people in the ways that I anticipated. Many of my peers asked questions about my time in the field. Some probed for more of the participants' insights. A few expressed anger about the program itself. After all, my professor, a well-published scholar in the field of educational leadership, suggested that I think about pursuing this project beyond the course. Based upon the study's findings, the school acted upon an aspect of its discipline policy that seemed to bear the most explicit racial undertones. As opposed to filing into the dining hall only after their peers got first dibs, students who have un-attended detentions now eat lunch together in detention hall, a small change to the program in the broad scope of issues it raised, but a sizable victory for the youth under its charge.

This exploratory study uncovered narratives of "bad kids" as expressed in a single public high school's discipline policy. For just a few months, I worked to expand the pilot as an alternative version of my dissertation to include a larger sample size, additional in-depth interviews, and more observational time at the school, but the limitations of such a study seemed to outweigh its advantages.

First, as a former employee and familiar face, my relationship to the school's administration and students may have enabled me to take observational fieldnotes, speak informally with students and staff, and generally move within the school building without arous-ing alarm to a researcher's presence or unnecessarily influencing the natural research setting. On the other hand, the administration's intimate role in shaping and facilitating the execution of the pilot and dissertation studies may have framed me as an apparatus of the administration. This perception would not have been far from the truth, as the administration's necessary involvement in the study, particularly in my quest to relocate former student interviewees and seek new ones, may have infringed upon my attempts to protect stu-dents' anonymity. Or, to take a different angle, if I developed rapport and trust with the students in my role as principal investigator, but changes to the Incentive Program since the exploratory study have remained miniscule, then resistance or lack of motivation to buy-in to the dissertation's value, to volunteer participation, or to share forthrightly would seem reasonable.

Second, on any given week, the pool of Orange Group students from which to select participants would be large, variable, and would lend itself to random or probability sampling, but I am not interested in causal relationships, predictions, or extrapolating findings to other situations, time periods, or people. These purposes are aligned with a positivist paradigm, whereas my goal is depth of meaning-making for students in their social spaces.

Third, I may learn much about what it is like to be considered a "bad kid" through an additional series of in-depth interviews and long-term observations of classrooms and detention halls, but this would neglect other important contexts that contribute to the social ecology of discipline.

Fourth, a questionnaire allowed me to impute response items, reduce them to numeric values, and disaggregate the data, but there is a problem with this. Even if the students or data gathered from other sources informed the subjective response items, the responses that I imputed in the pilot survey or may have inserted in an additional questionnaire for the dissertation are my own constructions, not the students' own words. "Bad" kids' own stories are what I am after.

Fifth, and most important to my purposes here, conducting this version of the dissertation certainly would have appealed to the sensibilities of conventional qualitative researchers, but the final product of covering my authentic interests in this way could only have shaped the lives of the people whom I ultimately hoped to touch indirectly and over time. More to the point, interrupting my brother's journey along the school-to-prison pipeline was an immediate concern, and I simply did not know how studying the Incentive Program could assist Chris in that moment. Even if it was only for 3 months, each passing day that I split energies between my continued work with my family and my attempt to expand the pilot into a dissertation, transferred acquired knowledge across projects, combined those discourses, and managed the contradictions among them, was not only crazy-making, but a waste of valuable time. By now, my brother was

looking into alternative education programs that required his willingness to leave school and our home for serious consideration. The
dissonance of my attempts to be in two places at once, intellectually
and often physically, and the rapid speed of my brother's decisionmaking process brought me back to where I began.

Variation Two—Undercover Lover: A Study of True Lies

In May 2008, I redesigned my dissertation to focus on Chris and
the meaning our family made of his school-leaving experiences, but
he would appear in the final write-up of this version as a composite
character in a story based upon my experiences as an educator and
my observations in schools. Merging my brother's life, as gleaned
from the observational records that I accumulated during my family visits, with my memories of other Black youth with whom I have
worked in schools, would allow me to do the interpretive work that
I originally proposed in a way that would draw attention to its par-
tiality, and conceal the relationship that gave me pause. Of course,
incorporating narratives of self and fiction presents a different set of
problems. It is one thing to posit the personal or explicate my sense
of self in another's story, but it is quite a different matter, it seems,
to recapitulate the selective experiences of others in highly personal-
ized tales of my own lived world. Critics of self-studies have accused
many scholars of giving up on writing about the "other" by writing,
instead, about themselves. In addition, the legitimacy of stories that
are fictitious as to person and perhaps place, but accurate as to practices and beliefs, has been debated. Under some conditions, however,
such accounts may be the only way in which an author can tell a tale.

Having conceded that the Institutional Review Board (IRB)
would find incredulous my family's communal efforts to protect its
rights and privacy, especially for the sake of my teenage brother, and
would either disapprove of the project or turn it "into a bureaucratic
nightmare" (Wolcott, 2002, p. 148), creatively disguising their identities was vital in order to keep the research afloat. In the end, by
determining that my study—with its emphasis on oral history and its
lack of generalizability—did not meet the definition of "research,"

the IRB did nothing, except dilute my argument for the legitimacy of alternative forms of presentation in the minds of some academics.

Exemption from the requirements for the protection of human subjects, "a series of steps and procedures designed ultimately to protect the institutions themselves" (Wolcott, 2002, p. 148), does not, however, provide relief from the guidelines of my own moral compass or accountability to the people who have agreed to participate in this project. As Wolcott (2002) makes plain and I firmly believe, "Ethics are not housed in such procedures" (p. 148). There are important ethical dimensions to intimate fieldwork and the publication of the details of my formal study, for which there are no clear instructions for handling, but that need to be acknowledged, troubled, and worked through.

The complex nature of my familial relationships, for instance, necessarily brought in an element of coercion. In addition to the potential personal and educational benefits of the project, I suspect that my family's willingness to participate was grounded, in part, in their interest of my own educational progress. Undoubtedly, completing the proposed dissertation in partial fulfillment of the requirements for a doctorate, the highest degree held by anyone in our family, was a common goal. For that matter, publishing this book will also be a shared accomplishment. Therefore, their concern for my well-being may have infringed upon their right to withdraw from the study at any time. Unfortunately, beyond reminding family members that they reserved this right to withdraw, I was at a loss for ways to deal with this issue. Small but steady monetary incentives may have also compelled family members, especially Chris, to participate. Our individual and whole-family meetings sometimes occurred at various places outside of our home (e.g., over coffee or dinner), the financial costs of which I often assumed; but, as long as family members knew that I was providing compensation for their time—not their responses—this arrangement should not have posed a significant problem.

Another good example of the ethical dimensions of my personal work involves the issues of informed consent and confidentiality. Although, for the dissertation, I did not draft and attain family members' signatures on an official permission-granting document, my intent to draw on information that I gathered in my capacity as a family member (e.g., sibling and daughter) *and* in my role as a researcher (e.g., participant-observer and interviewer) was always apparent. This does not mean that I used my familial access in ways that were deliberately stealthy, sneaky, or deceitful, such as rummaging through our family home for personal artifacts to advance my research agenda. However, this does mean that the family was aware of the converging character of my identities and agreed to grant me broad discretion to record observations and descriptions of relevance within and beyond our formal or scheduled talks.

To be clear, note-taking and reporting are two different actions, and I did not ask the family for free-rein authorship or permission to write anything that I wanted about them. As qualitative work often calls for, this study was collaborative at every opportune juncture. At least monthly, I disseminated copies of working drafts of the dissertation and met with the family to member-check or solicit feedback about the accuracy, completeness, and fairness of my treatment. Chris himself was satisfied with the developing drafts. Many of his exploits that I thought he might want deleted or at least subdued were unproblematic. His primary concern seemed to be that I might miss some important detail about such exploits that he deemed pivotal to any manuscript about him. Otherwise, during these debriefings, we decided what not to disclose, to rid copy of sensitive information, and to fictionalize particular details, determinations that I would have noted in the final write-up. As the research progressed, however, and as carving time out to reestablish expectations of and my respect for our privacy became part of the research process, we also began to question the usefulness of anonymity and to reassess the costs of candor. Six months into the development of the second version of my dissertation, together we redefined our own ethical code of behavior and decided to reveal ourselves to the public.

Going Public: On Uncovering

By October 2008, I had tired of finagling what we considered arbitrary methodological limits, and my brother was on his way to live at the Joliet, Illinois Job Corps Center in the hopes of attaining a high school equivalency certificate and tile-setting apprenticeship. Participating in and conducting the research, and sharing my interpretations of the information that I gathered over the course of a year with family in casual talks and in formal writings, helped us communicate more frequently and intentionally about understanding one another and resolving tensions surrounding Chris' trajectory. Despite our work together, though, Chris was convinced that even in his suburban, Black middle-class environment, public schools were too hostile, competitive, and isolating for boys like him, and that the family's efforts to keep him in this environment had made us complicit in his school failure. This aspect of my research purpose—keeping him around long enough to earn a diploma—at this point, would necessarily go unfulfilled.

Having peered into my brother's life for a year in search of clues about how he understood his own schooling experiences and how we—family members, educators, policymakers—could shape his life outcomes, I saw that Chris needed time and space to adjust to his new milieu, and I wanted the same to write. Over the next 4 months after he left, I used the unstructured interview, journal, and observational fieldnotes that I had accumulated over the year to construct a layered portrait of my brother—a Black middle-class school dropout—and his social contexts. Even though I was able to pull from a plentiful corpus of information to write, the story still lacked the insights of key family members who love and lived with Chris, as well as Chris' point of view in his own words. From February to April 2009, in total I conducted and transcribed seven additional in-depth semi-structured retrospective interviews with each member of our immediate family, and when he was ready, which did not turn out to be until September 2009, Chris began authoring and sharing his own life history with me. While he wrote for the next 2 or 3 months, I gathered and analyzed documents from the two communities where he was raised to juxtapose his story with a picture of the local neighborhood and school backdrops that worked on and through him.

To be sure, the better part of nearly 2 years that I spent "working the hyphens" (Fine, 1994) was complicated labor. Throughout data collection, I struggled to smoothly maneuver the thin lines between each of my identities (e.g., expert negotiator–supporter-child-peer-traitor–trusted loved one–sister-scholar-insider-outsider in my own home), and I cannot say with certainty that I performed any of these roles especially well. My researcher status, position to power, and relationships with participants not only produced multiple and simultaneous roles, but these issues surely had implications for what occurred in my presence, what I saw, and how others saw me. I engaged in casual family gossip with my sister and at the same time facilitated an unstructured interview. I answered telephone calls from a frustrated brother who simply wanted to vent and I wrote copious notes from the other end. I arranged times to chat with my mother, but felt awkward when she insisted on having them take place in our museum-like formal dining room that only gets used on special occasions. I formally interviewed my stepfather, but the transcript of this conversation was useless because of the background noise provided by the old-school records he was playing as we spoke. Doing this research provided the flexibility to wear many hats, but everyone in the family wanted me to put on each hat at different times and we could never predict (and I did not make it a practice of announcing) the moments when I swapped one in favor of another.

The intimacy between my family and me made "leaving the field" somewhat tricky as well. Typically, a researcher has a clear exit strategy, such as when research funding has been exhausted, when the themes of interest seem to have fully manifested, or when one's welcome in the community under study has worn out. Because working from home is relatively inexpensive, our lives keep changing, and I am always welcome to stay, when to draw a line in the sand was a difficult decision to make. I mulled over when to make the transition from researcher and all of its associations back to family member, and how to do it in a way that did not give a sense of finality to or abandonment of the work that we constructed together. Leaving the field, however, took on new meaning when, at times, Chris would not answer my calls, return my text messages, or otherwise make himself available to me as a researcher, particularly when he was angry and worried that I was in cahoots with another family member. Oddly enough, our intimacy made me—not my brother—more susceptible to desertion. Although his absence was often frustrating, I understood his need for a break. Being the primary participant, the center of the controversy, and the single source of insight about the under-researched school-leaving experiences of Black middle-class youth was a heavy load for such a young person to bear. I never perceived my home/work with the family to be exploitative or manipulative of my access, but this was (and still is) something about which I worry and converse with my family.

Another one of my incessant concerns has always been the personal risks associated with our decision to write up the final version of this qualitative dissertation as an explicitly unconventional approach to understanding school dropout. I knew that many audiences of people—education policymakers, education researchers, educators, parents, and youth themselves—connected to youth who are caught up in the school-to-prison pipeline could use a text that, as clearly and directly presented as possible, speaks to the broad significance of getting to know our kids in all of their particularity. Our parents' motivations for going public were as much about connecting with fictive kin (Stack, 1974) across the globe—relatives not by blood or marriage, but by social or economic relationships and reciprocal struggles to raise their sons—as it was about dispelling the stigmatizing myth of dysfunctional Black families, particularly as it impacts the efforts of Black mothers. Chris, too, wanted to disrupt the dominant narrative of "bad" Black boys that is typically associated with his poor and urban counterparts, but manages to permeate class and spatial locations, and he figured that by baring all, he could replace our mediated images with more realistic understandings of what it is like to be him. Still, I am apprehensive about my family's willingness to be so forthcoming, considering what such vulnerability can mean, especially later in my brother's adult life.

Resource List

If I had things my way, you would leave the final pages of this book invested and appalled, sympathetic and all riled up—perfectly positioned to consider what, exactly, can be done about the under-education of youth like Chris. To supplement my bibliography of readings that you ought to check out, what follows is a brief list of suggested resources: my thoughts on reliable places where educators can learn and do more.

Professional Organizations

American Educational Research Association
American Educational Studies Association
Coalition of Schools Educating Boys of Color
Critical Race Studies in Education Association
National Alliance of Black School Educators
National Association for Multicultural Education

Coalitions and Activist Networks

Association of Raza Educators (ARA)—San Diego
Dignity in Schools
Education for Liberation Network
Educator's Network for Social Justice—Milwaukee
Future Teachers for Social Justice—Chicago
Literacy for Social Justice—St. Louis
New York Collective of Radical Educators (NYCoRE)
Teacher Activist Group (TAG) National Network
Teachers 4 Social Justice (T4SJ)—Bay Area

Websites

Black Male Development Symposium, blackmaledevelopment
.com
Illinois Balanced and Restorative Justice, IBARJI.ning.com
Rethinking Schools, rethinkingschools.org/index.shtml
Schott Foundation for Public Education, schottfoundation.org
Teaching Tolerance, tolerance.org

Journals

Black Studies
Educational Action Research
Educational Researcher
Ethnography
Harvard Educational Review
International Journal of Qualitative Studies in Education
Journal of African American Males in Education
Journal of Educational Foundations
Journal of Negro Education
Narrative Inquiry
Qualitative Inquiry
Qualitative Research
Race Ethnicity and Education
Urban Education
Urban Review
Teachers College Record
Teacher Education Quarterly

References

Advancement Project, Padres and Jovenes Unidoes, Southwest Youth Collaborative, & Children & Family Justice Center of Northwestern University Law School. (2005). *Education on lockdown: The schoolhouse to jailhouse track.* Available at www.advancementproject.org

Alexander, M. (2012). *The new Jim Crow: Mass incarceration in the age of colorblindness.* New York, NY: The New Press.

American Educational Research Association (AERA). (2006). Standards for reporting on empirical social science research in AERA publications. *Educational Researcher, 35,* 33–40.

Ayers, W. (2010). *To teach: The journey of a teacher.* New York, NY: Teachers College Press.

Ayers, W., Dohrn, B., & Ayers, R. (2001). *Zero tolerance: Resisting the drive for punishment in schools.* New York, NY: The New Press.

Brant, B. (1994). *Writing as witness: Essay and talk.* Toronto, ON: Women's Press.

Brown, E.R. (2003). Freedom for some, discipline for "others": The structure of inequity in education. In K. J. Saltman & D. A. Gabbard (Eds.), *Education as enforcement: The militarization and corporatization of schools* (pp. 126–150). New York, NY: Routledge.

Catalyst Chicago. (2009). Reaching Black boys. *Catalyst Chicago, XX*(5).

Children's Defense Fund. (2007). *America's cradle to prison pipeline.* Available at www.childrensdefensefund.org

Civic Enterprises. (2006). *The silent epidemic: Perspectives of high school dropouts.* Available at www.civicenterprises.net/pdfs/thesilentepidemic 3-06.pdf

Civil Rights Project. (2000). *Opportunities suspended: The devastating consequences of zero tolerance and school discipline.* Available at civilrightsproject.ucla.edu/research/k-12-education/school-discipline/opportunities-suspended-the-devastating-consequences-of-zero-tolerance

-and-school-discipline-policies/crp-opportunities-suspended-zero-tolerance-2000.pdf

Coalition for Juvenile Justice. (2006). African American youth and the juvenile court system. Available at www.juvjustice.org/factsheets.html

Collins, P. H. (1994). Shifting the center: Race, class, and feminist theorizing about motherhood. In E. Glenn, G. Chang, & L. Forcey (Eds.), *Mothering: Ideology, experience and agency* (pp. 45–65). New York, NY: Routledge.

Dantley, M. E., & Tillman, L. C. (2010). Social justice and moral transformative leadership. In C. Marshall & M. Oliva (Eds.), *Leadership for social justice: Making revolutions in education* (pp. 19–34). Upper Saddle River, NJ: Pearson.

Davis, L. (2011, April). Improving correctional education for incarcerated adults and juveniles. Paper presented at a regional meeting of the Correctional Education Association, Effingham, IL.

Daza, S. L. (2008). Decolonizing researcher authenticity. *Race, Ethnicity and Education, 11*, 71–85.

DuBois, W. E. B. (1990). *The souls of Black folk*. New York, NY: First Vintage Books.

Dunn, L. M. (1968). Special education for the mildly retarded—Is much of it justifiable? *Exceptional Children, 35*(1), 5–22.

Ferguson, A. A. (2001). *Bad boys: Public schools in the making of Black masculinity*. Ann Arbor, MI: University of Michigan Press.

Ferri, B. A., & Connor, D. J. (2006). *Reading resistance: Discourses of exclusion in desegregation and inclusion debates*. New York, NY: Peter Lang.

Fine, M. (1994). Working the hyphens: Reinventing self and other in qualitative research. In N. K. Denzin & Y. S. Lincoln (Eds.), *Handbook of qualitative research* (pp. 70–82). London, England: SAGE.

Fine, M., & Smith, K. (2001). Zero tolerance: Reflections on a failed policy that won't die. In W. Ayers, B. Dohrn, & R. Ayers (Eds.), *Zero tolerance: Resisting the drive for punishment in schools* (pp. 256–263). New York, NY: The New Press.

Fine, M., Torre, M. E., Boudin, K., Bowen, I., Clark, J., Hylton, D., Martinez, M., Roberts, R. A., Smart, P., & Upegui, D. (2001). *Changing: The impact of college in a maximum-security prison*. New York, NY: The Graduate Research Center of the City University of New York.

Foucault, M. (1995). *Discipline and punish: The birth of the prison*. New York, NY: Vintage Books. (Original work published 1977)

Fuchs, D., & Fuchs, L. S. (1995). What's "special" about special education? *Phi Delta Kappan, 76,* 522–530.

Glaze, L. E. (2010). Correctional populations in the United States, 2009. *Bureau of Justice Statistics.* Available at www.bjs.gov

Goffman, E. (1963). *Stigma: Notes on the management of a spoiled identity.* New York, NY: Touchstone.

Gustavson, L. (2007). *Youth learning on their own terms: Creative practices and classroom teaching.* New York, NY: Routledge.

Harry, B., & Klingner, J. K. (2005). *Why are so many minority students in special education?: Understanding race and disability in schools.* New York, NY: Teachers College Press.

Hehir, T. (2005). *New directions in special education: Eliminating ableism in policy and practice.* Boston, MA: Harvard Educational Publishing Group.

Hinchey, P. H. (2008). *Becoming a critical educator: Defining a classroom identity designing a critical pedagogy.* New York, NY: Peter Lang.

hooks, b. (2001). *All about love: New visions.* New York, NY: HarperCollins.

hooks, b. (2002). *Communion: The female search for love.* New York, NY: HarperCollins.

Howe, K. (2009). Positivist dogmas, rhetoric, and the education science question. *Educational Researcher, 38,* 428–440.

Huppke, R. (2009). 1 child left behind. *Chicago Tribune.* Available at www.chicagotribune.com

Kunjufu, J. (2005). *Countering the conspiracy to destroy Black boys.* Chicago, IL: African American Images.

Lather, P. (1991). *Getting smart: Feminist research and pedagogy with/in the postmodern.* New York, NY: Routledge.

Laub, D. (1992). Bearing witness, or the vicissitudes of listening. In S. Felman & D. Laub (Eds.), *Testimony: Crises of witnessing in literature, psychoanalysis, and history* (pp. 25–30). New York, NY: Routledge.

Lopate, P. (1995). *The art of the personal essay: An anthology from the classical era to the present.* New York, NY: Anchor Books.

Losen, D. J., & Orfield, G. (Eds.). (2002). *Racial inequity in special education.* Cambridge, MA: Harvard Education Press.

Lyon, D. (2007). *Like a thief's dream.* Brooklyn, NY: powerHouse Books.

Marshall, C., & Oliva, M. (2010). *Leadership for social justice: Making revolutions in education.* Upper Saddle River, NJ: Pearson.

McNally, J. (2003). A ghetto within a ghetto: African-American students are over-represented in special education programs. *Rethinking Schools*

Online, 17(3). Available at www.rethinkingschools.org/archive/17_03/ght173.shtml

Meiners, E. R. (2007). *Right to be hostile: Schools, prisons, and the making of public enemies*. New York, NY: Routledge.

Mills, C. W. (1997). *The racial contract*. Ithaca, NY: Cornell University Press.

Mills, C. W. (2000). *The sociological imagination*. Oxford, England: Oxford University Press.

National Research Council. (2002). *Scientific research in education*. Washington, DC: National Academy Press.

National Research Council. (2004). *Advancing scientific research in education*. Washington, DC: National Academy Press.

Noguera, P. A. (2008). *The trouble with Black boys: And other reflections on race, equity, and the future of public education*. San Francisco, CA: Jossey-Bass.

Ong-Dean, C. (2009). *Distinguishing disability: Parents, privilege, and special education*. Chicago, IL: University of Chicago Press.

Oswald, D. P., Coutinho, M. J., & Best, A. M. (2002). Community and school predictor of overrepresentation of minority children in special education. In D. J. Losen & G. Orfield (Eds.), *Racial inequity in special education* (pp. 1–13). Cambridge, MA: Harvard Education Press.

Parrish, T. B. (2002). Racial disparities in the identification, funding, and provision of special education. In D. J. Losen & G. Orfield (Eds.), *Racial inequity in special education* (pp. 15–37). Cambridge, MA: Harvard Education Press.

Petit, B., & Western, B. (2004). Mass imprisonment and the life course: Race and class inequality in U.S. incarceration. *American Sociological Review, 69*, 151–169.

Ropers-Huilman, B. (1999). Witnessing: Critical inquiry in a poststructural world. *Qualitative Studies in Education, 12*(1), 21–35.

Said, E. W. (1994). *Representations of the intellectual*. New York, NY: Vintage Books.

Schott Foundation for Public Education. (2004). Public education and black male students. Available at schottfoundation.org

Schott Foundation for Public Education. (2010). Yes we can: The Schott Foundation 50 state report on public education and Black males. Available at schottfoundation.org

Shaw, C. (1966). *The jack-roller: A delinquent boy's own story*. Chicago, IL: University of Chicago Press.

Sheehan, S. (1993). *Life for me ain't been no crystal stair: One family's passage through the child welfare system.* New York, NY: Vintage.

Sheets, R. H. (1996). Urban classroom conflict: Student-teacher perception: Ethnic integrity, solidarity, and resistance. *The Urban Review, 28,* 165–183.

Skiba, R. J. (2001). When is disproportionality discrimination?: The overrepresentation of Black students in school suspension. In W. Ayers, B. Dohrn, & R. Ayers (Eds.), *Zero tolerance: Resisting the drive for punishment in schools* (pp. 176–187). New York, NY: The New Press.

Slavin, R. E. (1989). Students at risk of school failure: The problem and its dimensions. In R. E. Slavin, N. L. Karweit, & N. A. Madden (Eds.), *Effective programs for students at risk* (pp. 3–17). Needham Heights, MA: Allyn & Bacon.

Spring, J. (2008). *American education.* New York, NY: McGraw-Hill.

Stack, C. (1974). *All our kin: Strategies for survival in a Black community.* New York, NY: Harper and Row.

Tolbert, M. (2002). *State correctional education programs: State policy update.* Washington, DC: National Institute for Literacy.

Vavrus, F., & Cole, K. (2002). "I didn't do nothin'": The discursive construction of school suspension. *The Urban Review, 34*(2), 87–111.

Watson, N. (2002). Well, I know this is going to sound very strange to you, but I do not see myself as a disabled person. *Disability and Society, 17*(5), 509–527.

Weeks, C. (1967). *Job Corps: Dollars and dropouts.* New York, NY: Little, Brown Publishing.

Werner, D. A., Widestrom, A., & Pues, S. (2012). In B. D. Fitch & A. H. Normore (Eds.), *Education-based incarceration and recidivism: The ultimate social justice crime fighting tool* (p. 74). Charlotte, NC: Information Age Publishing.

Winn, M. (2011). *Girl time: Literacy, justice, and the school-to-prison pipeline.* New York, NY: Teachers College Press.

Winterfield, L., Coggeshall, M., Burke-Storer, M., Correa, V., & Tidd, S. (2009). *The effects of post-secondary correctional education.* Washington, DC: The Urban Institute.

Wolcott, H. F. (1983). Adequate schools and inadequate education: The life history of a sneaky kid. *Anthropology and Education Quarterly, 14*(1), 3032.

Wolcott, H. F. (2002). *Sneaky kid and its aftermath: Ethics and intimacy in fieldwork.* Lanham, MA: Rowman & Littlefield.

Index

About the Author

Crystal T. Laura is an assistant professor of educational leadership at Chicago State University, a comprehensive institution on the city's storied South Side. By day, she explores leadership preparation for learning in the context of social justice with the goal of teaching school administrators to recognize, understand, and address the school-to-prison pipeline. During the second shift, she coparents two marvelous boys who give her work in the field of education particular urgency.